THE STRANGEST
PLANTS
IN THE WORLD

THE STRANGEST PLANTS IN THE WORLD

Professor S. Talalaj
D. & J. Talalaj

ROBERT HALE · LONDON

ISBN 0 7090 4732 0

Robert Hale Limited
Clerkenwell House
Clerkenwell Green
London ECIR OHT

Manufactured in Singapore

Contents

Preface

This book has been written not only for plant admirers, but also for those with little knowledge of the wonders of plants. By selecting the most unusual plants and their incredible stories, we have tried to show how fascinating the world of plants is, once certain unknown facts are revealed.

Some plants are of particular interest because of their beautiful flowers, peculiar fruits or seeds, remarkable size or incredible age. Often, however, it is their 'hidden' qualities which make them so intriguing. Some plants possess an unusual ability to change human behaviour or induce euphoria and because of such remarkable properties, in the past they were believed to be gods. In fact, even human beings were offered as sacrifices at the altars of special temples, built to please god-plants. Furthermore, under the influence of secret plants, European witches in the Middle Ages claimed to be able to make mysterious flights to meet the devil. People were actually accused of witchcraft and executed at the stake, just for possessing such 'evil' plants.

Although some of these stories seem to be incredible, they are nevertheless true. It is hard to believe that under the influence of a certain magic poison containing plant ingredients, a shaman can change a man into a 'living corpse', a state of coma indistinguishable from death.

THE STRANGEST PLANTS IN THE WORLD also describes plants which were believed to be able to cure any illness or to restore sexual power to old people. Some plants were also considered to be an antidote to any poison. A ship full of precious goods was offered by a European king in exchange for just one nut from a plant of unknown origin, which was believed to have miraculous powers.

The reader will also find in this book stories of plants which 'behave' strangely, including those which have developed remarkable methods of catching insects and eating animal flesh. We even describe a flower which resembles a female insect and so invites male insects to copulate with it, thereby ensuring pollination.

Over one hundred of such strange plants have been described in this book and we hope their stories will fascinate the reader. We also hope that once the uniqueness of plants has been revealed, more people will learn to appreciate the value and beauty of plants. Tropical forests, home to many unique plants, are now diminishing under the axe at an alarming rate. Industrial timber operations expanding into virgin forests pose a real threat to many magnificent plants which may be lost for ever. Even the most remarkable *Rafflesia arnoldii*, the world's largest flower, is endangered in the tropical forests of Indonesia. We do hope that from now on the readers of this book will take the side of those trying to preserve the world's vanishing flora. We must support the dramatic appeal of the tribe living in the vanishing jungle of Sarawak: "You have the world, leave us the forest!".

The authors would like to acknowledge the help of their publishers, especially Michelle Anderson and Jamie Anderson, who polished this book to make it more attractive.

Adelaide, 1991

1.

Plants Used in Black Magic

Living Corpse

Since antiquity certain plants have been known for their remarkable power to kill, to heal, to cause fantastic dreams, to change perceptions of reality, or to induce a deep sleep. Not surprisingly, such plants were exploited by witch-doctors, shamans and witches who used them in 'black magic' and were thereby able to give the impression that they possessed powers equal to the gods.

In Haiti an application for certain plants was found that sounds incredible. The seeds of the thorn apple (*Datura stramonium*) and *Datura metel*, which are known as zombie cucumbers because of their fruits, were used as an ingredient of an unusual secret poison. This poison was used by certain malevolent local shamans or priests to change a man into a zombie, that is into a so-called 'living corpse'.

Anthropologists who worked in Haiti brought home fantastic stories about the existence of zombies long ago, but they were ridiculed by scientists as a product of the imagination. No-one took them seriously. But it has recently been revealed that these stories were in fact true. In a scientific report published in 1983 in the Journal of Ethnopharmacology, a real case of zombification was described from Haiti. According to this incredible report, in 1963 a young man suffering a mysterious disease was brought to a local hospital. He was in a critical condition; his blood pressure had dropped dramatically and his heart beat was extremely weak. In spite of medical help the man soon died. An official death certificate was signed by two resident doctors, and the man was buried in the local cemetery. It was a great shock to the community, the report says, when twenty years later, a middle-aged man approached a woman at a local market, introducing himself by the nickname of her deceased brother. It was a name known only to the most intimate family members. The man claimed that many years before he had been changed into a zombie by his brother who hated him. He claimed to have worked as a slave on a remote sugar plantation until the death of his master freed him.

This unusual case, treated initially with suspicion, was thoroughly investigated by doctors and the local police and confirmed as true. It has been revealed that the secret zombie poison was not given in drink form, but was applied directly to the skin of the victim by the zombie maker. As it causes severe itching, the victim scratches the skin and this

Thorn apple
Datura stramonium

Deadly nightshade
Atropa belladonna

facilitates the absorption of the poison. Under the influence of this poison, the victim's breathing becomes weak, and after a time his heart beat ceases almost completely. The patient looks dead so that even an experienced doctor can be misled and consider such a man to be dead. However, the victim of zombification is still alive. He falls into a deep lethargy, but retains consciousness and is fully aware of what is going on around him. But being paralysed he can do nothing. He can even hear the crying of his relatives during the funeral ceremony. When he is finally put into the grave, the buried man is still alive, and can survive on the small supply of air in the coffin.

Now, at a chosen moment, when nobody is around, the victim is secretly dragged from the grave by the zombie assistants. The zombie maker then gives his resurrected man a potion of *Datura* plants to drink to make him fully 'alive'. But the man, who is now called a zombie, is in a state of shock and, in the midst of the confusion caused by the *Datura* potion, he has no power to protest. He agrees to do what his masters say and is usually sold as a slave. Having experienced his own death and burial, mysterious resurrection, and being regarded as dead by all the community, the zombie is aware that his sudden appearance at home may frighten people to death. So, zombies normally work on sugar plantations and do not try to return home.

It is interesting that although *Datura* plants are the main active ingredient of the zombie poison, the incredible state of lethargy is induced by an animal poison. The zombie makers fortify the plant poison by adding an extract of the flesh of certain puffer fish (*Diodon* species), which is among the most toxic agents ever discovered. Zombie makers must be very clever specialists as lethal cases of zombification are very rare.

Little Gallow Man

Mandrake (*Mandragora officinarum*), a small herbaceous plant native to the Mediterranean region, has a peculiar root which can be likened to a human figure. People with imagination can easily distinguish a torso with legs and even sexual parts of the human body, with a typical female or male shape. This sexual appearance gave the plant its reputation as an effective sexual stimulant and it was used as a fertility charm. Another power of this plant was also soon discovered. A strong decoction or an extract made with wine was found to be an excellent pain-relieving agent. Such preparations were in common use as an anaesthetic in surgical operations long before ether was employed.

In ancient times, people were aware of another interesting property of the mandrake, which is its ability to induce a long and deep sleep. Hannibal, a Carthaginian general, the story says, defeated his enemies by exploiting the power of mandrake. When African troops rebelled against the authority of Carthage, the astute general pretended to retreat, but left behind many jugs full of wine, to which an extract of mandrake root had been added. When the rebellious soldiers arrived, they drank the abundant wine, fell into a deep sleep, and were easily overpowered by Hannibal's returning troops.

The power of mandrake to relieve the most extreme pain was also exploited during Roman times when people suffered torture on the cross. Mandrake wine was given to such victims by sympathetic women often just before their death, and was known as 'death wine'. But this death wine could have an unexpected effect. As mandrake wine induces a deep sleep with very shallow breathing and a weak heart beat, the crucified victim could appear dead when in fact he was still alive. At such moments, the victim was usually brought down from the cross and given to his family for burial. In such a way, the 'death wine' could save the victim's life. Some authors have even made the suggestion that Christ could have been given mandrake wine and so survived his torture on the cross.

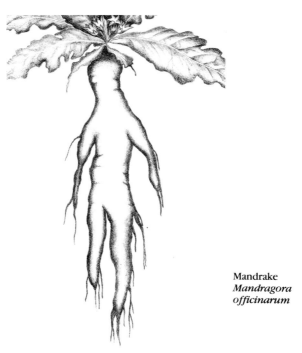

Mandrake
Mandragora officinarum

Belief in the miraculous power of mandrake was so great in the past, that it was used against plagues. It was said that neither demons nor evil spirits could bear the sight of the miraculous humanoid root. For this reason pieces of mandrake root were often used as amulets to ward off evil.

A peculiar cult based on this plant developed in Germany in the Middle Ages. A human-like figure of the mandrake root was wrapped in silky cloth and it was bathed every Friday as if it were human. The water in which the figure was bathed was collected and used as a remedy, particularly to relieve pain during child birth. This pagan cult was severely prosecuted and, it was said, three women were executed in 1630 in Hamburg alone for worshipping mandrake. Even Joan of Arc was accused of possessing a mandrake and this led to her torture and death at the stake.

In ancient Italy people used to bury a mandrake figure in the ground, with only the head exposed, and the magic root was believed to forecast the future. The mandrake figure was even believed to make a man who possessed the miraculous root invisible when under attack by his enemies.

Mandrake was claimed to be most difficult to find. It was said that it could only grow from the semen spilled from a man who was hanged for crimes he never committed. So, the plant was called the 'little gallow man'. To find a plant one had only to search under gallows. Even the collection of the root was considered a most risky job, as it was said mandrake would immediately kill those who tried to pull it from the ground.

People took elaborate precautions to protect themselves from the fury of revengeful mandrake. Wax had to be put in the ears so that the terrible cry of the dying plant would not kill the collector. The most popular method was to use a dog. The collector would tie the dog to the exposed root, and then throw a piece of meat in front of the hungry animal. Straining to get the meat, the dog would rapidly pull the root from the soil. The dog, it was said, would die in convulsions caused by the power of the dying mandrake. Little wonder that collectors demanded an enormous price for a piece of mandrake root. In fact, less honest collectors procured 'false' mandrake humanoid figures from other, similar plants.

As mandrake root in large doses can cause severe poisoning and hallucinations, it is now classed as a drug of abuse and its use is restricted by law.

Witches' Herb

Deadly nightshade, also called belladonna (*Atropa belladonna*), is among the most poisonous plants known. The name 'atropa' is derived from the name of the Greek goddess of death, whose sole duty was 'to cut the thread of life'. The name 'belladonna' literally means 'beautiful lady' but has another connotation. The plant juice, especially of the fruit, when applied directly to the eye has the power to enlarge the pupil of the eye. It was commonly used in ancient Italy by women who wanted to enhance their attractiveness.

No other plant found in Europe has such a strong connection with witchcraft as deadly nightshade. It was in fact regarded in the past as the property of the Devil. According to one fable: 'The Devil goes about trimming and tending it in his pleasure, and can only be diverted from its care one night of the year that is Walpurgis night, when the Devil is preparing for the witches' sabbath'.

Small wonder that with such a reputation, belladonna became an important ingredient of the famous witches' ointment used in their flight to meet the devil. Before the trip, a witch would simply rub her skin and especially her private parts with this ointment, then, sitting astride a broomstick, she was ready for a mysterious flight for intercourse with the Devil. It was the power of belladonna that made that mysterious flight seem a reality. One witch, when asked, admitted: 'I had a crazy sensation that my feet were growing lighter, expanding and breaking loose from my body . . . I experienced an intoxicating effect of flying.' Many witches claimed that they had participated in a joyful banquet, dancing and coupling with young men 'which they desired most of all'.

Witches were severely prosecuted in the Middle Ages for their evil practise, which were unacceptable to the Church. As a result of a Bull of Pope Innocent VIII of 1484 condemning witchcraft, over a million women were tortured and executed in Europe.

Belladonna was also famous for its power to kill and became an ingredient of secret poisons, which were used to get rid of unwanted persons or rivals to the throne. During the days of the Borgias, a potion of belladonna was kept hidden in various places in their palace, just in case. Poison was often secretly added to food, even to fresh fruit. It was risky to consume food in the company of eminent persons and there was even a saying in those days in Italy; 'Don't eat cherries with the Pope'.

When Duncan I was King of Scotland, Macbeth's soldiers poisoned the invading Danes by using a liquor mixed with belladonna extract supplied to them during a truce. After the invaders, who suspected nothing, drank the poisoned liquor, they were overpowered by the Scots.

Although the deadly belladonna plant contains substances which have an important application in medicine, it causes severe poisoning, and hallucinations, and it can easily become a drug of abuse. It is now restricted by law and can be used under medical supervision only. Some people still use this plant to experience a 'trip'—often with fatal consequences.

*Magic
Mushroom*

In ancient times people were puzzled by the remarkable growth of the fly agaric (*Amanita muscaria*), a well known, attractive but poisonous mushroom with a brilliant red and white spotted cap. Arising from an 'egg' after heavy rain, and rising fast like a sexually aroused human organ, fly agaric was even regarded as a replica of the fertility god himself. Small wonder that a mystery cult, in which this mushroom played an unusual role, developed in ancient times. The Aryans who came from the north-east to Afghanistan about 2000 years ago, brought with them rituals devoted to a god they called Soma. This god was, in fact, a fly agaric. It was worshipped by the sect's members as a god, and was not just a sacrament or a symbol.

Fly agaric achieved such an unusual level of veneration because of its remarkable power. Unlike other toxic mushrooms, this fungus, when ingested in small quantities, does not kill, but causes remarkable changes to perceptions of reality. It is known to induce powerful hallucinations during which fantastic worlds can be seen with closed eyes. Small wonder that in the past, fly agaric was used to communicate with the gods and spirits of deceased relatives.

Fly agaric
Amanita muscaria

The power of the fly agaric has long been known to Koriaki tribes living in the Siberian tundra. They must have discovered its power to invigorate sexual performance as it became a popular aphrodisiac. Women used to give such mushrooms to their husbands to help their love making. In Siberia these mushrooms were often collected in distant areas by men, but it was women who prepared the mushrooms for consumption. They were dried and then chewed and made into sausage-like quids a few centimetres long, which were easy to handle.

The precious mushrooms were so scarce in some districts that only the rich could afford to purchase them. But inhabitants of the Siberian tundra were clever enough to discover that the pleasure experienced by the wealthy could easily be repeated without money. The less fortunate, by simply drinking the urine of those who had already taken the drug, could achieve the same effect. An early account provides convincing evidence about this most peculiar practice: 'The poor sort, who cannot afford to lay in store of these mushrooms post themselves on these occasions round the huts of the rich and watch the opportunity of the guests coming down to make water and then hold a wooden bowl to receive the urine, which they drink off greedily and by this way they also get drunk'. We now know that the pleasure-inducing substances of this mushroom are excreted unaltered with the urine, and this is a unique quality among all hallucinogenic substances discovered so far.

Fly agaric, when ingested, is also known to cause a dramatic change to the perception of objects. Under the influence of this mushroom, a small crack becomes a creek, a tiny twig turns into a large tree, and a man of modest stature becomes a menacing giant. Consumption of a quantity of this mushroom also brings a feeling of unusual power and strength. In Scandinavia, in the past, soldiers were able to fight in a wild and fearless frenzy for a long time without fatigue after eating this mushroom.

A bizarre concept of the power of this mushroom is expressed in a small church in Indre in France. A fresco on the wall shows Eve encountering a serpent entwined around a giant fly agaric. This painting evidently suggests that it was not an apple but the fly agaric mushroom which was offered by Eve to Adam in paradise.

It should be noted that fly agaric, which is used to kill flies, is a deadly poison to humans when ingested in an excessive dose. Cases of lethal poisoning, especially among children, have been reported.

God-plant of Gabon

Iboga (*Tabernanthe iboga*) a shrub native to equatorial Africa, is among the most famous plants in this category. Its root is regarded as a most effective sexual stimulant, more powerful than the famous yohimbe used in many parts of Africa. A decoction made from the root bark is used in religious ceremonies, especially in Gabon, during which the power of the plant enables people to speak and hear spirits of their ancestors.

Among the members of the Ubangi, a secret society in the Gabon region, the iboga root is known as Bwiti and regarded as miraculous, and worshipped in religious ceremonies. Before an applicant is admitted to this secret society, he must meet the god-plant Bwiti, which is achieved by using the plant extract. As the amounts drunk during such initiation ceremonies are large, some applicants are fatally poisoned as a result. All-night parties are held during which iboga plant decoctions are drunk both by the priests and the society members, with songs and compulsive dancing. Such ceremonial dances are organised by the priests who prepare the potion from the root. It is not only drunk, but also chewed to enhance the drug effects. Everyone is given a chance to see the Bwiti, their god, as the plant has strong hallucinogenic properties. Frenzied dancing makes the people thirsty, so they often rush to a water source and drink large draughts of water and continue their compulsive motions as if in a trance. Some of these dances resemble epileptic fits more than ordinary dancing.

The miraculous root is believed to have the power to reveal the place where objects have been hidden by ancestors. There is a common belief in Gabon that if such hidden treasure is not found this may cause the sudden death of a family member.

As well as this miraculous plant's strong stimulating power, another interesting property has been discovered by the natives. When used in a certain dose the iboga root causes an entirely different, if not 'opposite', effect. The people utilise this drug in hunting. Under its influence the hunter becomes so calm that he can remain absolutely motionless for many hours.

2.

Plants Used in Human Sacrifice

Sacrificial 'Table'

An unusual application was found in ancient times for a peculiar barrel-like cactus (*Echinocactus grusonii*), native to deserts of Mexico. Shaped like a huge barrel some 130 cm tall and 1 m wide and densely covered with strong spines, up to 5 cm long, ancient Aztecs found this plant most useful during human sacrifice. When a chosen victim was placed on this 'sacrificial table' his body was severely injured by numerous needle-like spines, and as a result the victim bled profusely and suffered horrendous pain, for the god's pleasure. Before he died the priest quickly cut open the victim's chest with a knife and removed the still palpitating heart to be offered in the temple as the greatest gift to a chosen god.

The most common was the sacrifice made to the sun god, Huitzilopochli, who was considered the most powerful among the Aztec gods. This god was believed to have conquered the moon and created the sun, a source of life, for his beloved people. To give him the power to keep the sun rising every day after the darkness of the night, it was necessary to provide him with human flesh and blood. This is why human sacrifice was considered the solemn duty of every mortal. Sacrifice and torture was not regarded, in those days, as a barbaric act, and it was a normal religious ritual accepted by everyone. It was considered an honour to be chosen as a sacrifice to the gods and those chosen were treated with great respect.

As the number of people to be sacrificed ran to thousands, it was usually a custom to use prisoners of war for the purpose. But at times when there were no wars with neighbouring tribes, special prearranged skirmishes were organised between members of their own community. Prisoners taken during such internal wars provided sufficient candidates for sacrifice. As the word for blood in the Aztec language also meant 'flower' such wars became known as 'flower wars', but they meant blood and not the bloom of the flowers.

The famous barrel cactus, which is the thickest among cactuses, also serves another less bloody purpose. Its juicy flesh can be used as a source of both food and water in an emergency and so the giant cactus may be a life saver in remote deserts where water may not be easily found. An American pilot said he survived when he had to abandon his plane in the Mexican desert because the barrel cactus provided him with water and food before he was rescued.

Barrel cactus
Echinocactus sp.

Century plant
Agave sp.

Bloody Crop   Certain plants played such an important role in the life of ancient people that many died for their sake in the past. Such is the incredible story of the common maize (*Zea mays*) which was a staple food of the ancient Aztecs. This plant was also held in great esteem by the ancient Inca civilisation in Peru.

The plant was so revered that in the Inca palaces special artificial maize gardens were created. Full size plants were sculpted from silver and gold and they were the main attraction for the noblemen.

Maize also played an important role in ancient religion in Mexico. Tlaloc, the Mexican god, was always represented in sculptures or paintings with a stalk of maize in his hand. In order to be sure of the gods' blessing on their maize crops, people deliberately sacrificed their lives to them. A special chapel dedicated to the powerful god of maize, named Cinteutl, was established in one of the most famous temples in Mexico.

As soon as the maize plant started to appear in the field, the ceremony related to this plant commenced. People used to go to the field where the best shoot of maize was chosen. Taken to the temple by the priest, this plant was treated as if it were a god. Food was offered and it was worshipped at the altar by the people until the maize grew in the field and was ready to be harvested. The harvest was also a special event. To assure a successful harvest the god had to be pleased by a human sacrifice. For this purpose, the most beautiful girl among the youngest was chosen. Ceremonially treated for some days, the girl had to be beheaded by a priest in a special ceremony, and her head offered in the temple to the powerful god of the maize harvest. But this was not the end of the story. As the maize storage was under the command of another god, another girl had to be offered. This god must have been even more demanding as the victim had to be skinned and the skin offered at the altar by the priest. Only in this way was the vital crop believed to be assured.

Gods themselves gave their people the best examples. Red Tezcatlipoca, the god of fertility, for instance, was voluntarily skinned alive to provide the life-sustaining maize crop for his people whom he loved and as a result the ancient Mexicans included skinning their own people in their religious ceremonies. In one ancient Aztec temple alone some 100,000 human skulls were found.

It is interesting to note that ancient people developed excellent methods of maize cultivation to ensure the best possible harvest. Some techniques now regarded as rather peculiar have survived in central America. For example, on the coast of Peru fish is used in maize growing. A farmer may be seen making holes in the soil to which, together with a few maize seeds, he adds a fish head to help the plant to germinate and grow.

Maize is a gift of America to the Old World, and it was first seen by Columbus in Cuba when he landed there in 1492. As the story says,

'A kind of grain called maiz, of which was made a very well-tasted flour' was brought to him by the natives.

Plant of Self-Sacrifice

The agave plant (*Agave* species) is a well known ornamental plant cultivated in gardens for its rosette of fleshy leaves rather than for its huge inflorescence which seldom appears. Agave leaves are equipped with sharp spines at the top, which may be lethal to grazing animals, and in this way the plant fights for survival. In ancient Mexico, agave leaves were a source of deliberate suffering for many people. As sacrificial offerings of one's own blood were common in ancient times, the priests, and often ordinary men, induced bleeding to offer at the altars of a chosen god. The sharp-as-a-needle agave became almost a weapon of self-torture in those days. The 'needle' was used to pierce the chest, arms, earlobes and often genitalia to induce profuse bleeding. Some gods were evidently satisfied with this 'modest' sacrifice, which did not involve the death of the victim.

In ancient Mexico this plant was not only a source of suffering, it was also considered to be one of the most useful plants in the country and became known as the 'miracle of nature'. The buds which appear at the base of the flower stalk, which may measure 50 cm across, were slowly baked in large stone ovens for many days and used as a staple food. The baked bud was sometimes pounded to form flat cakes, and stored for times of need. When the flower stalk rose from the rosette of the leaf, often up to 6 m high, the natives simply bored a hole in the middle of the stalk and tapped the exuding sap into a container. After fermentation, it became a common alcoholic drink. The method was invented by the ancient Aztecs and became their favourite drink, called pulque. It was used during religious ceremonies and it was held in great esteem, which is borne out by the fact that the priests recognised four hundred different gods responsible for pulque. A goddess of fertility, Mayhuel, was represented as a woman with four hundred breasts, and she was also worshipped as a goddess of pulque.

It is of interest that the use of this drink was strictly controlled as it was considered to occasionally become a 'whirlwind, a cyclone that covers everything with evil'; evidently a result of drinking excessive quantities. Children and the young were forbidden to drink pulque, but the old and those who survived a calamity or recovered from disease could drink pulque at will.

The traditional use of pulque has survived in Mexico, and at present many thousand agave plants are used solely for this purpose in Mexico. It became a national drink, consumed in thousands of small bars around the country known as pulquearias. Mexicans show their gratitude to this unusual plant and respectfully call it the 'tree of marvels'.

Agave plants are also famous for their pattern of blooming. No-one knows when they will raise their huge flower stalks. Some agave plants need twenty, some forty and even sixty years to be ready to bloom. But once the plant produces its huge inflorescence which looks like a tree, the plant becomes exhausted and dies. Another interesting feature of this plant is that apart from flowers it also bears small bulbils, which are miniature plants. When they fall from the flower-stalk they take root and give rise to the new plant. In Europe, where this plant is often grown in botanic gardens, it blooms so rarely that its bloom is announced in the media and people rush to the garden to see its remarkable inflorescences.

It was formerly believed that the plant bloomed only every hundred years. This is not true, but the name 'century plant' has survived.

3.
The Routes to Paradise

Sacred Cactus

When Spanish conquistadors arrived in Mexico, they were astonished by a peculiar cult among the native Indians, in which a plant played such an unusual role. It was peyote (*Lophophora williamsii*), a small cactus which has the power to change perceptions of reality, when ingested. The Indians dried the cactus and button-like pieces of it were used in their religion as a kind of holy communion. Under the influence of such communion, a man could see breath-taking pictures of fantastic and unreal worlds. He would experience prolonged hallucinations during which he could see coloured visions of mysterious objects with strange geometric designs. It is no wonder that a plant with such an unusual effect was regarded as a road to paradise. In fact the visions caused by the plant were commonly regarded as glimpses of heaven.

Peyote
Lophophora williamsii

Central American Indians searched for the marvellous cactus, often in remote regions, making long and exhausting trips. The whole community waited for their return as this meant a time of excitement and joy for all. With the new supply of the wonderful peyote they could be happy and dance for hours without fatigue.

The peyote plant was mostly used in religious ceremonies, and since such ceremonies were spreading dramatically and accepted by other Indian communities, Spanish Jesuits were alarmed. With this powerful peyote cult, there was little chance to introduce Christianity to the new land. A special law prohibiting the use of peyote was passed by the Spaniards in 1720, but this only resulted in the sacred plant being used in secret.

The cult based on the use of peyote also developed in the USA among the Indian communities. The American authorities tried to eradicate the movement, but soon the battle was won by the plant worshippers. Finally a special church known as the native American church was officially established. It is a peculiar mixture of Christianity and paganism, as peyote still remains a holy sacrament in this church. Only members of this church are allowed to consume peyote, which is forbidden in other regions.

Investigations have revealed that the small cactus, which is only about 5 cm tall, and spineless, contains powerful mind-bending substances. Ingesting such cactus causes changes to perceptions of reality, and occasional use for a 'trip' may lead to addiction, which may result in serious deterioration of health, and is difficult to cure. One physician who experienced the action of peyote wrote: 'I saw jewellery . . . and wonderful carpets gleamed in a thousand fires. They then transformed themselves, before my eyes, to flowers, to butterflies and glittering wings. With every second that passed I was regaled with new forms.'

Because of the great demand for wild-growing peyote for its official 'eaters' in America, the plant which was once abundant, now faces extinction. It only survives in a few areas north of Rio Grande.

Some authors suggest that the principal poison the plant contains is there as a repellent to predators, but nature did not foresee that man would find the tiny plant so attractive to eat that he would become its most deadly enemy.

Flesh of the God

Since ancient times a tiny mushroom (*Psilocybe mexicana*), native to Mexico has been known for its remarkable power to change perceptions of reality. The ancient Aztecs called this mushroom the Teonanacatl, which literally means, the 'flesh of gods'. Its action is most unusual. When ingested it causes a peculiar feeling as if the body and the spirit had separated, and anyone who eats it can see fantastic scenes from an unreal world in continuous colourful visions. Little wonder that in ancient times this mushroom was held as a sacred plant. An anthropologist who studied the effects of this mushroom reported: 'When they chew this mushroom, they are beginning to be excited. They start singing, dancing and weeping. Some see themselves dying in a vision, others see themselves being eaten by a wild beast, others imagine that they are capturing prisoners of war, that they are rich and possess many slaves . . .'

In Mexico, in ancient times, when the gods had to be provided with human flesh as a sacrifice, the use of this mushroom was of particular importance. After cruel ceremonies of decapitation or killing on the spiny cactuses, when the sacrificial table was literally covered with human blood, people who took part in such ceremonies were often exhausted and depressed. The miraculous mushroom brought some relief to the spectators of sacrificial ceremonies.

The feasts which followed the consumption of the tiny mushroom were not always the happiest of events. Under the influence of this mind-changing plant, some people became aggressive and ready to fight without evident reason, and, the story says, many died by their own hands on such occasions. It was said that it was 'a devil who spoke to them'.

Mushrooms which cause a feeling of unreality have also been found in other countries. In Australia mushrooms of the same genus can sometimes be found growing in the woods. Young people occasionally consume the tiny mushrooms to experience a 'trip'. It should be pointed out that these mushrooms are highly poisonous and cases of severe poisoning in those who risked their lives and ingested such mushrooms have been reported in Australia in recent years. We should be aware that such hallucinogenic mushrooms may even grow in the vicinity of our house, in the lawn. It was reported that a three-year-old girl was admitted to hospital suffering a kind of intoxication and other peculiar symptoms, but no reason for this 'illness' could be established initially. It was the girl's mother who finally noticed that the girl was fond of some tiny mushrooms growing in the lawn. Investigations revealed that the mushroom the girl frequently consumed was a *Psilocybe subaeruginosa* known for its strong mind-altering properties.

'Joy' Plant

The power of the opium poppy (*Papaver somniferum*) to relieve pain, to reduce troubles and induce an unforgettable state of well-being, has been known since antiquity. Sumerian tablets found in Mesopotamia and dating back to 4000 BC mention the opium poppy, which was referred to as a joy plant. Homer in his Odyssey, sings of opium which 'lulls pain and permits to forget sorrow'. The origin of this plant is connected with many fables. According to one legend Buddha was once so overtaken by sleep that he decided to cut off his eyelids to prevent it. These, the story says, fell to the ground whereupon the famous sleep inducing plant appeared.

From the unripe fruits of the opium poppy a milky juice is obtained by cutting the surface with a knife. The exuded latex hardens to yield opium. Opium has remarkable power and it became a drug of abuse in

Hallucinogenic
mushroom
Psilocybe sp.

Angel's trumpets
Brugmansia candida

the Orient, especially in China and India. Opium was commonly smoked for pleasure, usually in special pipes, and often a special procedure was employed. Some opium is usually heated over a flame at the end of a stylet until a small ball of the roasted opium is formed. This mass is then pushed into a pipe head and in such a way it is ready to be smoked. In another technique a small piece of opium is held over a live charcoal and the smoke formed is simply inhaled. Although the actual smoking is short, lasting some 1-2 minutes only, the lungs have a large absorption capacity so the effect of intoxication by opium is almost immediate.

The great demand for this pleasure-inducing drug resulted in great trade in opium. It was such a lucrative trade it even had an impact on the history of some nations. It is very unusual for a bloody war to erupt because of a dispute over a plant, but the opium poppy was the cause of such an outbreak. A disagreement between China and Great Britain led to the so called Opium War in the 1830s. The Chinese, who became concerned about the dramatic spread of the dangerous habit of opium smoking, decided to prevent its import. However, this threatened the interests of the British who dominated the opium trade with China. As a result of hostility the first Opium War erupted in 1839 between England and China and lasted till 1842. The British won the war and as a result five Chinese ports were opened to Britain, and Hong Kong island was transferred to the British. This did not, however, end the dispute over opium trade. A second Opium War erupted in 1865 and this time it forced the Chinese to accept British conditions.

Smoking opium induces fantastic visions and is very pleasurable, but the craving for the new experience is so intense that an addict may resort to violence and crime in order to get the drug. Intoxication is followed by a deep sleep, but when the smoker awakes from the mysterious and unreal world, reality becomes hell. The man may be so sleepy after waking, that he may dislocate his jaw by yawning. He may cry copiously but they are not the tears of joy this time as the addict often suffers most unbearable abdominal pain and intense diarrhoea as a horrible side effect. He may pass sixty stools a day and his body is shaken by involuntary twitching he cannot control—small wonder that such behaviour is described by opium users as 'kicking the habit'. One should bear in mind that the horror of withdrawal from opium abuse is unparalleled. As one physician treating such addicts commented: 'God forbid that the reader of this book should ever know from direct experience what the addict suffered . . . a shattering experience, and even a physician finds it an ordeal to watch the agonies of patients in this condition'.

Opium and its main hallucinogenic component morphine are classed as hazardous habit-forming drugs, and they can only be used under the supervision of a doctor.

It is remarkable how an important and beneficial medicine, such as morphine, which has saved millions of soldiers on the battlefield from horrific pain, may become a menace when improperly used or used just to make an 'innocent' trip.

Deadly Coca

The remarkable power of the leaves of coca (*Erythroxylon coca*) has been known since antiquity. This shrub or small tree grows wild in the Andean highlands of South America. People must have soon discovered that by chewing coca leaves they could forget their sorrows and become happy.

Various legends are associated with the discovery of this plant. According to one, a tribe living in the highlands of the Andes, known as Younga people, was punished by the powerful god of snow for their misdeeds, by banishment. The people left their land and tried to find refuge in the higher mountain regions. But as there was no food or drink there was little chance of survival. One of the members came across a shrub and to relieve his hunger he started chewing its leaves. He immediately became strong and active so the other members did the same. Thanks to the remarkable power of coca to relieve hunger and thirst, these people, the story says, crossed the most treacherous mountains with ease.

During the times of the Incas coca leaves were regarded as a gift of the gods to the people, and the plant was used in religious ceremonies. People could not afford to use this plant on a daily basis and it was only the privilege of members of the royal family and noblemen. It was customary in those days to place a branch of coca in noblemen's graves to ensure that they would not be thirsty or hungry.

When Spanish conquistadors arrived in Peru they soon learned about the use of coca leaves by the native Indians, and the unusual power of this unique plant. They did not use the leaves themselves, but took advantage of the plant for their own purposes. They started to provide coca leaves regularly to the people working in their gold mines. In return, the people who customarily chewed coca worked more efficiently. As coca makes people happy despite miserable conditions, by providing coca the Spanish had no problems with strikes among the workers. It is thanks to coca-chewing that porters of Peru can carry huge loads in high altitudes despite a lack of oxygen. They can work all day without fatigue. They just replenish the quids of coca with new leaves from time to time. Just by counting the number of quids they used during their trip, they measured the time without a clock. Similarly, an excellent postal system operated in Peru in the past, which was based on runners and was so efficient due to the constant use of coca leaves.

Coca was unknown in Europe, and it was first introduced in the nineteenth century. An Italian physician, Angelo Mariani, used coca extract from the leaves imported to Europe to make the wine called Vin Mariani a more potent drink. As such fortified wine had strong mind-altering effects, due to the hallucinogenic action of cocaine, little wonder that his business was a great success.

Probably the most successful commercial use of coca leaves is that of the famous Coca-Cola drink. Although the main plant ingredient of this beverage is obtained from the seeds of the African cola plant the extract of coca leaves was also important as it made this drink narcotic and addictive. When in 1904, the dangerous narcotic property of cocaine was recognised, the US authorities were forced to order the Coca-Cola producer to change the famous beverage by removing the coca. Coca-Cola retained its trade name, but the extract which is used now no longer contains the dangerous coca alkaloids, and it only gives its specific flavour to the drink which is now regarded as entirely safe.

Although coca seems to be a beneficial plant in Central America, there is probably no other plant in the world that causes more misery to those people who try coca or pure cocaine and then cannot fight the dangerous habit. Habitual use of coca causes horrendous health deterioration, and thousands of people die as a result of chronic use of cocaine in western countries. The craving for another dose of this narcotic drug is so strong that an addict is ready to commit crime and murder to get the drug. Illicit smuggling causes great danger to the people of the USA, as billions of dollars worth of cocaine has been smuggled from Central America. The USA sent its troops to Colombia in 1989 to fight the trade in the deadly plant.

The most vulnerable to this dangerous drug are young people who self-confidently assume that they will only try the drug and then not repeat the experience. But there is sufficient scientific evidence that in most cases one experience with a hard drug leads to continuous use, and this is the reason that all governments in the world try to prevent the use of coca, now a deadly plant for humans.

It must be noted, on the other hand, that cocaine is a powerful medicinal agent and has been used to relieve pain. Coca plant was a source of an important analgesic, which still has its place in medicinal practice. The chemical structure of cocaine served as a model for synthesising new, more efficient and non-addictive analgesics.

Plant of the Assassins

The unusual mind-bending power of cannabis (*Cannabis sativa*), also called Indian hemp, has been known since time immemorial. In ancient Mexico, the Aztecs used the cannabis plant in their religious ceremonies, especially during human sacrifice to please the powerful god of fire, named

Huehueteotl. The story says that the prisoners of war to be sacrificed to this god at the top of the sacrificial platform in the temple, were first stupefied by using cannabis. The powdered plant was simply thrown in large amounts into the faces of the prisoners who ate the powder and became intoxicated. When considered sufficiently numbed, they were then thrown one by one into the naked flame of the ceremonial fire to be burned alive. But before death could intervene and put an end to the agony, a priest quickly cut open the breast of the victim with a sharp knife. The heart of each victim was then removed and offered to the god of fire.

In the thirteenth century, habitual users of cannabis were hired to commit political murder. Such groups of people, who were ready to commit any crime to get cannabis in return, were known as 'assassins'. This name derived from the Arabic word 'assassassin' meaning fanatical courage. These people were known for their remarkable courage in fighting and killing.

The use of cannabis for pleasure was a common habit among the Scythians some 2000 years ago. When they wanted to forget their sorrows, for example after a funeral or a calamity, they used cannabis which they believed had the power to take away misery from their souls. They used to gather in a tent, in which powdered cannabis leaves were thrown on glowing stones. Sitting around the stones they simply inhaled the resulting smoke, and were said, 'to be seized by an ecstasy of joy'.

Not only smoking but also eating cannabis with honey or jam or even mixed with butter is known. Whatever the method used, it always produces a kind of well-being and change to perceptions of reality, so it acts as a typical hallucinogenic drug. It is sometimes called a 'leaf of delusion'.

In some parts of Africa the use of cannabis is very common, but it has a special religious connotation for the Baluba tribe. These people chose this plant to be their great spirit and leader and they have become a special sect of cannabis users. They destroyed the fetishes they used to worship and turned to cannabis, in a strong belief that this remarkable plant would alter their miserable lives and bring happiness. Remarkably, their religious rituals are now based on the consumption of cannabis. Members of the peculiar sect believe that cannabis has the power to remove any misery or calamity from the whole tribe. Ironically, when a man commits misdeeds, he is punished not by having to abstain from the use of this plant, but by being forced to use it in overdose. He must smoke several cigarettes of cannabis one after another. The result is considered to produce such an unpleasant effect that the man will learn a lesson.

The Zulus in South Africa smoke cannabis in a different way. They mix some dried cannabis leaves with dried dung, cover it with earth and make two holes in a hip form. Lying on the ground in front of the holes, they eagerly inhale the smoke, with evident pleasure.

The sticky resin of the plant contains powerful hallucinogenic substances, and it mainly occurs in the female flowers. Collection of cannabis resin differs according to the region. For example, in some regions it is obtained by squeezing the plant tops between the palms of the hands. In other regions a collector wears thick leather garments, and by walking through the field all day, the resin sticks to the garment and can be scraped off later.

As occasional use of cannabis to induce a 'trip' may lead to addiction, and this causes health deterioration, its use is illegal in many countries.

Pituri

First European explorers penetrating the desolate Simpson Desert of central Australia, noticed that the Aborigines living there had a peculiar custom of chewing the leaves of a certain tree they called 'pituri'. The leaves were collected from a small native tree, *Duboisia hopwodii*. The native Australians who lived in the harshest conditions had discovered that chewing the leaves of this particular plant helped them forget their thirst and hunger and made them happier. The Aborigines roasted the leaves over a low fire, moistened them with saliva, and rolled the leaves to form a plug, which would be carried behind the ear and used when necessary.

The dried leaves of pituri were also mixed with the ash of a certain acacia plant, and the mixture was believed to be more potent. As the ash has an alkaline effect, it released the active alkaloids in the plant so it could be absorbed and this was a real improvement invented by the Aborigines.

Some European explorers who met Aborigines shared pituri with them, and this was regarded as a most friendly gesture. The explorer King, a member of the famous but tragic Burke and Wills expedition and the only member who survived, admitted that it was chewing pituri that enabled him to survive. He said by chewing pituri with the Aborigines whom he met, he became 'perfectly indifferent to his miserable conditions' and could survive, while the other members died of starvation. Although pituri caused some intoxication, however, it was the fact that he shared it with the natives who must have also given him their food which helped him to survive.

But pituri is not only a reliever of hunger and thirst, it is a strong hallucinogen. It is interesting that initially only the elders of the tribe were allowed to chew pituri. The powerful plant helped them to maintain their privileged position within the community. Under the influence of pituri, they claimed that they could communicate with the spirits of their ancestors and were able to forecast the future.

The use of pituri spread later to other communities in Australia but the plant does not grow in many regions where Aborigines lived. Those who had the plant in their vicinity started to collect the leaves and take them to other areas. As a result pituri became an important article of trade among the Aboriginal tribes of Queensland. The collectors could easily swap their famous leaves for any product they needed such as shields or boomerangs.

Those who had pituri trees near where they lived did not use the leaves to experience the plant's effect. It was customary to make a small hole in the trunk, pour some water in and insert a stopper. A strong liquor, ready to drink, would be found in the hole the next day.

The Aborigines were aware of the highly toxic effect of this plant when used in large doses. Emus were an important source of food among many tribes. and they used the plant to help catch them. They placed the leaves in a waterhole to which they knew the emus usually came. It was a simple but efficient method. Once the emus drank the poisoned water they did not die but they could not escape as they had become strongly intoxicated. They behaved rather like a drunken man, slowly walking in circles instead of straight, and so were easy to catch.

Poisoning of waterholes in the lands 'visited' by the Aborigines was so common in the past, that those who did not know about it could easily be killed by drinking the water. In 1874, one explorer who must have experienced this danger, tried to warn other travellers in Australian lands. He said: 'People travelling would be wise to avoid using water from these drinking places, or small holes of surface water, as the blacks often put in some preparations to stupefy emus'. Even large animals often became the prey of this powerful poison, and for this reason the Aborigines in some parts of Australia call the pituri tree camel poison.

Flower of Paradise

The discovery of the famous khat (*Catha edulis*), also known as Arabian tea, is connected with many legends. According to one, it was discovered in Yemen. A humble shepherd once noticed that his goats, having eaten leaves and branches of a certain plant, became unusually excited and alert. He decided to check this effect on himself. Before going to sleep he consumed a twig of this plant and waited for the result of his experiment. The result was astonishing, he lost all tiredness and desire to sleep and the whole night, the story says, he could meditate without fatigue.

The plant has the power to enliven the imagination, clear ideas, cheer the heart and remove the desire to sleep. Initially this plant was used mainly by the elderly who were able to pray longer during the night by chewing fresh khat. But soon its use spread to whole communities in Arabic countries. It became customary to chew khat during religious ceremonies and during weddings and funerals. Some people chew khat from dawn to dusk and some even chew it all night.

The use of khat was common in Ethiopia in the past, especially in the villages. Depending on the amount of khat consumed the emotional stages of khat users could be clearly distinguished. In the first stage, they said, in the early morning before using khat, a man felt frustrated and unhappy. In the second stage, when he had started chewing khat, he began to smile. In the third stage when he had chewed a lot, he forgot all his troubles and worked the whole day happily, without fatigue.

Little wonder that this plant was often called the 'flower of paradise' although only the twigs and not the flowers were used.

Only fresh khat is considered to be effective, and it is common to see khat sellers sitting in the streets of Middle Eastern towns and in East Africa. The seller sets a good example by chewing khat and occasionally spitting.

An application has also been found for khat in powdered form. The elderly who have weak teeth prefer using powdered khat rather than chewing tough twigs. Such powdered khat is mainly offered to the elderly before their long pilgrimage to Mecca.

In Harara district, the only region from which khat could be obtained in the past, the plant was believed to have other virtues. It was not only regarded as an excellent stimulant, better than coffee, but was regarded as an excellent cure for almost any illness. It was said that khat could cure 501 diseases. This corresponded to the numerical value of the Arabic word for this plant Ga-a-t, which is exactly 400+100+1.

Although the effect of khat is usually likened to that of a strong cup of coffee, most khat users say that they experience much more. Khat contains some substances which have hallucinogenic effects. In some countries khat is classed as a drug of abuse and health authorities warn that using khat may lead to addiction as it is highly toxic if used in great excess. Some people become aggressive under its influence, and grave injuries among habitual khat users were occasionally reported, but such cases are rather infrequent.

Intoxicating Pepper

Among plants of Oceania which have become famous is kava-kava (*Piper methysticum*), known as kava or intoxicating pepper. It is a herbaceous plant, the rhizomes of which have been used since ancient times for making a special drink, commonly known as kava-kava. Early European explorers who were offered this drink were reluctant to accept it as they knew how it was prepared. They noticed that the kava rhizomes were first chewed by young girls and boys who sat around a large container, and while constantly chewing the rhizomes, spat into the jar. The plant material obtained in such a peculiar way was mixed with water and it was then ready to drink.

The drink is of such ceremonial significance in Fiji and Tonga that an important visitor is offered kava-kava on entering the house or office. It has a long tradition in Oceania and its origin has many legends. According to one Tongan fable, a chief called Loak once travelled to a small island to see his former attendant named Fevanga. As it was a time of famine the attendant had no food to offer his eminent guest. In despair he decided to secretly kill his leprous daughter, cooked the flesh and served it to his visitor. But the chief quickly recognised what it was and he refused to eat the meat. He ordered it to be buried in the garden. Fevanga did as he was ordered and in this place a plant grew up with remarkable properties which could relieve sorrow.

When used in a normal dose this drink is a stimulant and causes a sense of well-being and laziness. It is customary to sit around a bowl full of kava-kava for many hours, till late at night, and the jar is empty. The custom of kava-kava drinking is regarded as a national pastime in many Polynesian islands. It is said that everyone drinks kava-kava. But while the noble class drinks it only for pleasure, priests drink it for religious purposes, and ordinary men drink it to relax.

Kava drink was unknown in Australia but in 1982 this custom was brought by Australian Aborigines from Fiji. The use of kava-kava has spread unexpectedly among many communities of Aborigines in the Northern Territory. Whole families, including children, spend hours sitting around a bowl full of kava drink. As a result children are often found sleepy during school, and adults became lazy and do not look for work. Any frustration which arises is easily relieved by the famous drink of Oceania.

Some people who drink a lot of kava-kava are known to experience a kind of hallucination but whether kava-kava is a hallucinogen is still controversial. Cases of poisoning from excessive use do occur but are rare. Early white explorers described the results of kava use as horrific, saying that 'people lose the use of their limbs, fall and roll about the ground until the stupefaction wears away . . . entire body trembling paralytic accompanied with the disability to raise the head'. Such stories were of course a great exaggeration typical of travellers who wanted to impress their listeners, but heavy drinking of kava-kava is known to lead to health deterioration.

It should be noted that the method of making the drink by chewing the rhizomes common in the past has now been replaced by more hygienic methods. The rhizomes are simply powdered prior to use and the drink is formed by mixing the powder with cold water.

Mind Bending Spice

It is hard to believe that a common spice such as the nutmeg (*Myristica fragrans*) when ingested in an excessive dose can cause the most dramatic effects. Its hallucinogenic properties were known to ancient Hindus as an Ayurveda script called this spice 'madashaunda', meaning narcotic fruit. Nutmeg has rarely been used alone in India, it is usually mixed with other narcotic plants such as betel to increase its potency when chewed. Powdered nutmeg is an ingredient of a herbal mixture sold in Africa by Hindu shopkeepers for chewing as a stimulant. It is called paan in Kenya and a different mixture is prepared for men and for women.

We once had a peculiar experience in our laboratory when a paan sample was brought by one of our students to examine. We found that it contained sliced betel nuts, anise and nutmeg. But when I started to chew the mixture to describe its taste I suddenly had a peculiar feeling that the wall of the laboratory had extended and become concave as if I was in a balloon. I was unable to move for a few minutes and the intoxication lasted about twenty minutes. As the paan sample was one for women, those for men must have given even stronger effects. We came to the conclusion that the effect was a combination of both nutmeg and betel.

As nutmeg is freely available as a spice it has occasionally been used, especially by youths to obtain a 'trip'. But the experience of such a trip is not pleasant. One student admitted: 'I began seeing visions when I closed my eyes. I was thirsty and lethargic all the next day and I had a bad headache. I have no desire to repeat the experience'. People who have taken large doses of this 'innocent' spice have become seriously ill, needing hospitalisation. Some of them behaved in an uncontrollable way. As one physician who treated a case of nutmeg poisoning said: 'The man exhibited the appearance of a snarling dog. Upon being questioned, he would retreat his head back into his neck, tighten up his neck muscles, retreat his tongue and bare his teeth. Upon awakening, he was terrified and asked if he were going to live or die'.

Nutmeg as an easily available narcotic drug does not cause serious social problems because the side effects which follow are so unpleasant they discourage its use. But the use of nutmeg is common among some prisoners, especially in the Caribbean region. Prisoners place the powdered spice on a heated foil and then inhale the fumes.

Nutmeg was once regarded as an important medicine. The aromatic nutmeg oil was used to fumigate streets, especially in Rome during festivals and the coronation of emperors. Nutmegs were believed to have the power to prevent diseases and were used in medieval Europe during the Black Death.

The plant that bears nutmegs was initially only found in the Moluccas, known as the Spice Islands. The Portuguese, who had a monopoly on the lucrative trade, tried to keep the price of this spice very high.

They used to destroy whole ships carrying the precious spice to maintain prices and to prevent the establishment of plantations elsewhere.

The Portuguese monopoly on nutmeg was later broken by the Dutch, and their monopoly was then broken by the British, so the history of this spice is fascinating. When the British established a nutmeg plantation in Malaya, export of viable seeds was strictly prohibited. To prevent the cultivation of precious nutmeg elsewhere, a strict law was enforced. If a native was found to have such a tree on his farm he would be severely punished. But despite this law, some nutmeg trees were discovered in the villages by British inspectors and the unfortunate owners could not explain who had actually planted the forbidden tree. It was later found that it was not a man but a pigeon, which was guilty. The birds were attracted by the pear-like fruits, ate the fruit and swallowed the hard nutmeg. The nutmeg was then excreted with their faeces. From such seeds the new nutmeg trees started to grow and the local people were stunned when police found a nutmeg tree growing on their land.

It should be noted that in very small quantities, when used as a spice, the plant is harmless, but if one or two seeds are eaten it becomes a deadly poison.

Angel's Trumpet   The unusual properties of the plants of the genus *Brugmansia* (also known as *Datura*) have been known by South American Indians since antiquity. They must have noticed that a concoction from these plants has the mysterious power to induce visions and a state of happiness. The plants, which are shrubs or small trees, are most attractive when in bloom and are covered with showy, trumpet-like flowers, often up to 25 cm long, *Brugmansia*s are called angel's trumpets because of these spectacular flowers. They are grown as ornamentals in warmer regions throughout the world, including Australia.

Various *Brugmansia* species have been cultivated in South American regions, especially in the Andes, and became the most popular narcotic agents of South America. Different parts of the plant are used and the potions are especially popular with shamans who claim that during the colourful vision they experience, they cross the border in to the mysterious world of spirits and are able to communicate with their ancestors. They are believed to prophesy the future of tribal affairs, diagnose diseases and apprehend thieves.

Brugmansia potions have occasionally been used as a correctional medicine in a belief that during the visions they cause, the forefather's spirit would lecture recalcitrant children. In some regions of Peru *Brugmansia* extract is given to children not to cure them but in the belief that they would be guided by the miraculous plant and would be able to discover gold. In Peru the native Indians believe that the potion made from the *Brugmansia* plant can reveal treasures preserved in ancient graves, hence the plant is often called the grave plant.

In southern Colombia the plants are associated with an evil spirit. People believe that the *Brugmansia* plant 'has a spirit in the form of an eagle which is so evil that if a weak person stations himself on the foot of the tree, he will forget everything'. Small wonder that this unique property has been exploited in a tribal initiation ceremony. Drinking *Brugmansia* potion became an essential part of initiation among the Indians, especially of the western Amazon region. During the initiation, which may last several days, each boy must drink a *Brugmansia* concoction, and he must not refuse any of the drinks offered by each community member. As it is physically impossible to drink so much, a peculiar alternative has been developed. The liquid is simply injected into the boy's rectum by means of a tube. As a result of such a double application the boy falls into a deep sleep. It is believed that during the visions he experiences he receives messages from his ancestors which explain to him how to change into a man. It is believed that during his sleep the boy will forget his past childhood and become a real man. He is now allowed to take a wife and can participate in the full activity of the tribe.

Concoctions of these hallucinogenic plants were also used in the past in another rather macabre ceremony, especially in Colombia. Powdered seeds of *Brugmansia*, added to a drink known as chicha, were offered to the wives of dead warriors so that in a stupor they could be buried alive to accompany their husbands.

Drinking *Brugmansia* potion is not a pleasant experience, because of severe adverse effects such as nausea, convulsions and even temporary insanity. Some people become so violent that they can hurt themselves badly and have to be overpowered by others. Some people experience terrifying visions of being attacked by deadly beasts and poisonous snakes.

Despite this, *Brugmansia*s are regarded as a gift of the gods, although 'not the agreeable gift of the gods like peyote and hallucinogenic mushrooms'.

In some regions of Colombia *Brugmansia* trees are planted as an adornment in cemeteries and are often called death plants. In fact the plant is very dangerous and may become a killer, especially when abused in an attempt to make a 'trip'. One man in Australia made a bad 'trip'. He was found dead in the bush after eating some fresh flowers collected in the garden. It is hard to believe, but this attractive plant is in fact a formula for death.

4.
Plants That Kill

A Deadly Tree

The first travellers returning from Java told incredible stories about the upas tree (*Antiaris toxicaria*) having the power to kill those who approach it. They claimed that this tree exudes a fume which is so toxic that even a bird flying over its canopy becomes poisoned by its fumes and drops dead. Resting under such a tree, they said, is very risky, and those who fell asleep under it would never wake. The plant was said to kill all plants surrounding it. Bones of animals and humans were often found under upas trees.

Although such stories were found to be false, the tree is in fact among the most poisonous plants known. Its sap has been used as an arrow poison and its power to kill is considerable. Natives who learned the skill of using arrows from childhood, became real experts in the use of such weapons. By blowing an arrow from a long wooden tube they could easily hit a target and inflict a deadly blow on an animal or a man. A man hit with such an arrow, often from a distance of 90 m, was usually mortally wounded.

Sir Charles Brooke described the power of the weapon during his expedition to Malaya: 'Before one hut there lay a fine strapping fellow, having just breathed his last. I waited to look at the body, as he seemed only to sleep. He had been struck in the chest by an arrow, which left no more mark than the probe of a pin. After receiving the wound, he dozed off to wake no more, and died half an hour after he was struck.' As another author reported: 'The effects are almost instantly fatal. I have been in . . . a boat when a man was struck in the hand; the poison ran so quickly up the arm that by the time the elbow was green the wrist was black, and the man died in about four minutes'. Thousands of Portuguese, Dutch and British died from arrows poisoned with the upas tree extract, while exploring Malaya.

The poison made from the upas tree was also used in Malaya in the past as a method of execution. In 1776, this poison was employed to put to death thirteen of the king's concubines on the grounds of infidelity to the monarch. The story says that the girls were lashed to posts, their breasts bared, and a sharp stick covered with upas tree extract lanced their breasts. All the women died within five minutes suffering great agony.

The poison is made by first making an incision in the trunk. The latex which exudes from the bark is collected, and then heated on a slow fire so that it becomes a thick waxy brown extract. In some regions the poisoned arrows are fortified immediately before use by dipping the poisonous dart in lime juice carried in a small container. As the lime juice is acidic it causes the poisonous substances to be released more quickly and in this way the arrow poison becomes even more deadly. The head of each poisoned arrow is strongly barbed, usually with sharp fish bones, to make a deeper scratch on the living target.

It should be mentioned that Friar Odoric, who travelled to Java in 1321-1322, was the first to describe this deadly poison to the West. It was not investigated however, and some 400 years later reports still indicated 'Under the tree itself no plant or grass grows . . . the soil is sterile, dark, and as if burned. Such poisonousness does the tree exhibit that from the infected air birds perching on the branches are stupefied and fall dead'. We now know that this was an exaggeration, especially when some reports warned 'No man dare approach it unless his arms, legs and head be protected by clothes'.

Ordeal by Poison

The calabar bean (*Physostigma venenosum*) is a shrub native to the coasts of Nigeria. It is famous for its large seeds, resembling horse-beans, for which an unusual application has been found in Africa. In some parts of West Africa the plant is believed to have the power to prove the innocence or the guilt of a man accused of serious crime or witchcraft. During a special meeting of the tribe the accused man is forced to drink a strong potion prepared from the calabar bean, which is a very potent poison and usually kills when ingested. There was a strong belief that after applying this poison the divine power would give its verdict. Anyone who was guilty would die and the innocent would survive. Many people died as a result of such an unusual trial and during their colonial rule in Nigeria, British authorities issued a special law prohibiting the deadly and unjust practice.

But a reputable African pharmacologist gave me an explanation which is worth mentioning. According to him there is some sense in such an unusual judgement. He said that a man who really was guilty of a crime would be convinced that he would die and would certainly be hesitant about drinking the potion and so would sip it bit by bit. Such an administration causes severe poisoning and death is inevitable. But an innocent person, he said, would not hesitate and believing in the justice of the ordeal, would drink it quickly and cause violent vomiting. Much of the poison would then be eliminated and the man had a chance of survival.

To prevent even such a small chance of surviving the ordeal, in some cases the poisonous extract was not only applied orally but also given to the victim in the form of an enema to double the effect.

The powerful poison attracted the interest of a white missionary who smuggled some calabar beans to Europe. As a result an alkaloid known as physostigmine was isolated and it became a useful drug in the treatment of eye diseases such as glaucoma. The British had problems obtaining sufficient quantities of this plant, as the natives wanted it for their own purposes and kept its whereabouts a secret. They even used to eradicate whole areas covered with this shrub to stop Europeans getting the seeds.

As the calabar bean resembles the horse-bean, it was occasionally taken as an edible seed and eaten—with horrible effects. On one occasion children stole a bag of beans from a ship about to leave for England. Having eaten the beans many children became seriously poisoned and several died.

There is another plant in tropical Africa for which a similar application was found. It is the tree (*Erythrophleum suaveolens*) which is commonly known as the ordeal tree as the poison obtained from its bark was also used to establish the guilt of a person accused of crime in Ghana. But in this case the concentrated bark extract, which is highly poisonous, is placed under the eyelid of the accused person. The poison, which is quickly absorbed through the eye, causes death from heart failure. This ordeal gives no chance of survival so someone accused is sentenced to death even before trial. This cruel method was formerly applied only to those who were accused of witchcraft, and many people died as a result. This strange method of judgement is now totally abandoned.

Killer Prayer Bean

The prayer bean (*Abrus precatorius*) is a tropical climber and is famous for its very attractive seeds. They are brilliant red with a distinct black spot at one end. The seeds of this plant have often been collected and used as necklaces or rosaries, especially in Buddhist monasteries—hence the common name for the plant—prayer bean or rosary pea.

These attractive seeds, however, are one of the most poisonous substances ever discovered. One seed, when eaten, is sufficient to kill an adult. Little wonder that in India the seeds of this plant have long been used as a secret poison.

The way the poison is applied is unique. To prepare the poison the dried seeds are crushed into powder and then water is added to form a pulp. The dish containing this pulp is left alone so that the water evaporates and after a time tiny crystals of poison appear. These crystals, which form as small needles, are composed of a pure abrin, toxalbumin, which is a powerful poison. When the skin of a victim is pierced with one of the needles, the powerful poison is absorbed. The shot is lethal. The prick is so slight that it may be taken as a 'bite' of an ant or mosquito, and may even remain unnoticed. The victim dies and there is no sign

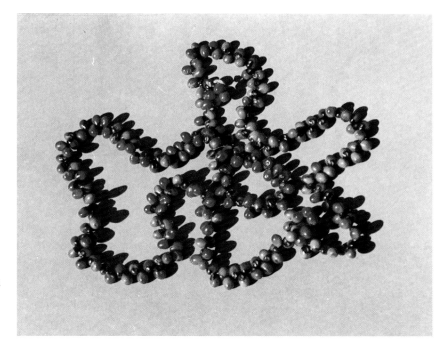

Necklace from the
seeds of the Prayer bean
Abrus precatorius

Oleander
Nerium oleander

of any injury, so the death is attributed to natural causes and is never detected. Almost an ideal poison, indeed.

The toxic abrin may also be dangerous when rosaries of the seeds are used as necklaces, especially on children. Not only is there a possibility that a child may eat the partly broken seed and be poisoned, but there is another risk too. The poison may enter small skin abrasions from the holes which were pierced to make the necklace. Because of this hazard, children should not be allowed to wear the necklaces at all. But sometimes a child may swallow a seed and not be poisoned. This is because the seeds remained whole and passed through the digestive tract without the poison escaping. But if the seed is chewed there is a danger of lethal poisoning.

An interesting feature of the whole plant, which is often cultivated as an ornamental in the tropics, is that it is extremely sensitive to changes in weather conditions, especially to any slight changes in 'electrical potentials' in the environment. Experiments performed in Kew Gardens in England indicate that the prayer bean may be useful in predicting such calamities as cyclones and earthquakes. But these observations are not yet accepted as scientifically sound, and are even ridiculed by some scientists.

In the past, prayer bean seeds were used as weights because the seeds are very hard and have a remarkably uniform weight of some one carat each. They were used particularly in Ghana for weighing gold and jewellery. The diamonds of India were evaluated by using this method of weighing.

Herb of the Queen of Hell

The most dangerous European plant is the famous monkshood (*Aconitum napellus*). This is a herbaceous perennial with attractive, deep blue, helmet-shaped flowers which may be likened to a monk's hood—hence the common name of the plant. The plant is so attractive that it has often been grown in gardens as an ornamental. When looking at this plant it is difficult to imagine that it is so dangerous.

Its poisonous properties have been known since antiquity. For instance, a spear smeared with an aconite root extract became a powerful weapon in battle as a simple scratch caused severe poisoning. Many battles in ancient Europe are said to have been won due to this powerful plant. The strong potion of the aconite root was used as a secret poison and in ancient times it was considered a crime even to own this plant.

In Greece, old people who had become a burden on the state were given a deadly drink of aconite. Small wonder that this dangerous plant was dedicated to Hecate, the Queen of Hell, in ancient times.

The aconite root was once used in Europe to poison wolves, hence its other common name, wolf's bane. Animals are aware of the poisonous properties of the aconite plant as neither rats nor mice attempt to eat it, even if food is scarce.

The aconite root is also related to witchcraft and was used, along with various vision-inducing plants such as belladonna, to fortify the effects of an ointment used by witches in medieval Europe. Not only did they claim to fly and have intercourse with the Devil, but they also insisted that under the influence of the magic ointment, they could be changed into wolves. They claimed they felt their bodies being covered with hair. These reports, which were ridiculed as evident lies, should now be revised. Experiments using alkaloids isolated from this plant have shown that they irritate the skin nerve endings in a most peculiar way causing a feeling of hairs rising on the skin. The witches were quite sincere when they told of their incredible experiences as a result of using the secret ointment.

Flying Death

Early travellers returning from South America brought unusual stories about Indian tribes living in the Amazon region, who could kill using poisoned arrows, hitting their target with great precision from afar. Even with their powerful guns, the first Europeans did not always win their battles with Indians. Many Europeans died and it is little wonder that they used to call the arrows 'flying death'. They could not learn what the poison was as it was a carefully guarded secret of the Indian tribes. The natives were proud of their deadly weapon: 'We know that white people know the secret of a black powder, but it has this disadvantage that it makes too much noise and frightens away the animals; our curare kills without noise, and no one knows from which direction the arrow came.'

Indians were also dangerous when fighting without arrows as they put the poison beneath their fingernails and a small scratch was sufficient to introduce the deadly poison in hand-to-hand fighting.

Preparation of the poison, which was called 'urari' and literally means 'he to whom it comes dies', was a secret guarded by tribal priests. It was prepared by boiling crushed bark of the tree until a sticky, blackish substance was obtained. It was usually kept in calabashes or bamboo tubes. The potency of the poison is checked in a peculiar way. If a monkey hit by an arrow coated with this poison is able to jump one tree only before it falls dead, the poison is classified as being 'one tree' of potency. If it can cover two trees it is still potent, but if the monkey can jump three trees the poison is too weak.

Spanish conquistadors who learned about the secret curare poison and saw birds killed with an arrow, considered the possible use of such a weapon for hunting in Europe.

The plant *Chondodendron tomentosum* which was commonly used for making curare is a small tree native to South America.

While Africans use bows to shoot arrows, in South America the tiny arrows are blown with great force from 3 m long bamboo tubes called by Europeans 'death tubes'. Practising from early childhood, an Indian can hit his target from a distance of up to 90 m. A small animal hit by such an arrow falls dead without making a noise. As the curare poison acts only when entering the bloodstream, the meat can be eaten with impunity.

Late in the sixteenth century, samples of curare were sent to Europe, but it was some 200 years before its powerful paralysing effect was investigated in 1743. Almost 200 years later, an alkaloid called d-tubocurarine was isolated. It has become an important medicine to relax muscles before surgical operations. In a proper dose the dangerous poison has become a very useful drug in modern medicine.

St Anthony's Fire

In the tenth century AD people in some European countries became victims of a mysterious disease from which thousands died in great agony. At that time no one could relate this disease to any plant. Whole villages were often affected, and in southern France in 994 AD some 40,000 people died after suffering horrible pain. Some victims suffered the feeling that their entire bodies were consumed by fire and others literally lost their limbs as a result of developing gangrene. The victims of this plague sought help in Egypt where St Anthony had organised a monastery to comfort the victims of the disease. Hence it became known as St Anthony's Fire.

This dreadful disease, for which no cure or prevention was known, had a profound influence on the course of history. In 1772, Peter the Great of Russia, who marched with his great army against the Turks, had to abandon his strategic plans because of a massive outbreak of the disease in his army.

It was not until the beginning of the nineteenth century that it was discovered that a plant caused the mysterious disease. The spores of a fungus, *Claviceps purpurea* attack ripening heads of rye, and cause a hard, horn-like, blackish-blue outgrowth to develop called ergot. When ergot-contaminated grain is used to make flour for breadmaking, the bread becomes toxic. As bread was a staple food, the amount of poisonous substances from ergot was sufficient to cause chronic poisoning.

It is interesting that when people frightened by the plague flocked to churches many of them were miraculously saved. We know now that it was actually a change in diet which saved them. In the churches and convents white wheaten bread was used and not fungus-contaminated rye bread, and so the poisoning eased dramatically as a result of the change of diet.

Acocanthera sp.

Glory lily
Gloriosa superba

It should be noted that poisoning by ergot-contaminated bread can also cause changes of behaviour as the plant has strong mind-altering effects and hallucinations are a common symptom. In a trial of witches in Salem, Massachusetts in 1692, twenty innocent girls accused of witchcraft were executed after trial. As the reason for their strange behaviour was unknown they were thought to have a pact with the Devil. We know now that it was ergot which was to blame for the verdict passed on innocent and suffering girls.

We are now aware of the danger of using ergot-contaminated grain and care is taken to remove the fungus from the grain after harvest.

Some poisonous alkaloids which occur in this tiny fungus have become useful drugs and are used in modern medicine. Some have the power to stop bleeding after childbirth, others are useful for the treatment of severe migraine. One of the substances isolated from ergot led to the synthesis of LSD, a powerful and dangerous hallucinogen and well known drug of abuse. After the discovery of LSD, its properties were kept secret for some time, as it was considered to have become a chemical weapon. It was thought it could be used to make an enemy defenceless and completely change his pattern of behaviour in the case of a superpower confrontation.

LSD is a strong mind-altering substance and its prolonged use causes severe chronic poisoning and even death. It is a typical addictive drug, so it is on the list of prohibited drugs world wide.

Deadly Rose Bay

Oleander (*Nerium oleander*) is a handsome shrub or a small tree native to the Mediterranean region, where it is called rose bay. This plant, with its attractive flowers, is often grown in gardens as a decorative plant. Those who enjoy its beauty often do not bear in mind that they are looking at a dangerous plant. It is deadly poison and all parts including the flowers are highly toxic and cause death to the unwary. Its deadly properties have been known since antiquity. During his famous Persian campaign, Alexander's army lost numerous horses poisoned by oleander. The water they drank was poisoned by the retreating soldiers placing oleander leaves in it. Some soldiers who used sticks of oleander to skewer their meat, became seriously ill and could not take part in battle.

Although cases of poisoning by ingesting oleander are rare, nevertheless they occur in Australia, especially among children who chew the flowers. Even adults are sometimes confused with the plants they use. In 1986 an Australian woman made an infusion of the leaves of deadly oleander, evidently mistaking it for similar elongated leaves of eucalyptus. This mistake in identification cost her her life. She could not be revived from the severe heart failure the poison caused.

The oleander plant is not only hazardous by itself. The plant, as a small tree, can become a host to mistletoe (*Viscum* species) which grows on its branches as a semiparasite. The mistletoe absorbs poisonous glycoside from the host plant, and if the mistletoe is used for medicinal purposes, the results could be horrendous. Mistletoe is a well known high blood pressure-reducing herbal medicine. This indicates how carefully plants which are to be used medicinally should be selected.

The deadly oleander however does not harm certain insects. There is a Danaid butterfly (*Danaids* species) which even takes advantage of the poisonous properties of the oleander. This butterfly is known to suck the deadly sap from the leaves and makes a peculiar weapon to repel its predators. It stores the poison in special cells, and keeps the poison just in case. Birds who attack other insects quickly learn that such butterflies are poisonous. After eating the insect they suffer great pain and vomit profusely. This seems to be sufficient warning to other birds to avoid this 'horrible' prey. Certain other butterflies which are not immune to the poisonous oleander juice take an entirely different approach. They simply change their colouration to resemble the Danaid butterflies, and this mimicry works as birds avoid them too.

Certain grasshoppers living in the Middle East where oleander is a common shrub, suck the juice of the plant and store it in a special gland from which, in cases of emergency, they simply stupefy the enemy by ejecting a stream of poison. A very interesting example of animals exploiting the power of plants.

There is some evidence that oleander exudes poisonous substances into the air and burning it in the fireplace can cause severe poisoning.

African Arrow Poison

The invention of the bow and arrow is among the most important made by man. It gave him a weapon with which he could kill an animal with accuracy at a distance. Primitive man was an expert in utilising poisonous plants and so arrow poisons were soon developed. Smearing an arrow with poisonous plant extract made it a potent lethal weapon.

Among the most common plants used for this purpose are various species of *Acocanthera*, especially *Acocanthera shimperi*, a small tree with an attractive white bloom. It is the most commonly used arrow poison in East Africa and its property was discovered accidentally by a woman in Kenya. According to legend, a poor woman found that her children became ill after eating some fruit, and one day she noticed a dead bird under the same tree. She took an ordinary arrow and rubbed it with the juice from the fruit and gave it to her son to hunt with. Although he only slightly wounded an animal it fell dead immediately. In this way the arrow poison was discovered and so the whole tribe was able to hunt even the largest beast and became rich, the story says.

Normally the root of *Acocanthera* is split into pieces and boiled in water and then such ingredients as snake's heads or lizards are added to 'fortify' the poison. As Emil Pasha described it in 1894, the preparation of arrow poison was as follows:

> The arrow poison is prepared by the learned man far from the village in the full secrecy of the forest. He cooks the powdered root . . . of the tree together with bark and adds lizards, snakes' heads, snakes' teeth and other dismal ingredients . . . After some time, the pot is removed from the fire and the poison which now forms a dark pulpy mass is allowed to cool overnight.

Arrow poison has remarkable killing power when introduced into the blood. A man would normally die in about half an hour just from being scratched with an arrow. The amount of poison found on one single arrowhead is sufficient to kill 250 people. Small animals would die after a short period of time while the poison takes several days to kill an elephant.

The potency of the arrow poison is often checked before use. A small amount of poison is introduced into the leg of a small tortoise. If the animal dies before walking five steps, the potency of the poison is correct. If, however, the animal only voids faeces as it walks and does not die, the poison is considered too weak and has to be remade.

Although arrow poison is mainly used for hunting, it is also known to be a secret homicidal poison. When used criminally, the method is very cunning indeed. The spiny fruit of the common plant called caltrops (*Tribulus terrestris*) is used for the purpose. The fruits are soaked in the poisonous extract so that the spines are covered with poison. When such fruits are spread on the path on which the victim is likely to walk home barefoot, the poison is easily injected as if from tiny syringes. A victim might think that it was an ant bite, but it was in fact a deadly blow. A victim has no chance of surviving and usually dies quickly. The death is usually attributed to snake bite or other 'natural' causes.

In some areas, e.g. in Kenya, the use of poisoned arrows for hunting is prohibited because of poachers depleting animal populations. A person found carrying poisoned arrows, especially in the bush, can be prosecuted.

Arrow poisons are rarely used in Africa in battle, but occasionally fights break out among certain tribes especially when gangs of cattle thieves make their raids in the Masai land in East Africa. According to a report which appeared in the *Daily Nation* in March 1972: 'A gang of cattle thieves armed with bows and arrows made a daring raid on the home . . . at the weekend and made away with 15 head of cattle after shooting and seriously injuring one person.'

It is customary in some parts of East Africa to poison machete tips or spears and they are usually used by Masai watchmen.

Drinking Smoke The tobacco plant (*Nicotiana tabacum*) was known to American Indians long before Columbus saw it for the first time. When he landed in Cuba in 1492, he was astonished by a peculiar habit involving this plant. He said that they burned the dried tobacco leaves in a kind of hollow reed, and inhaled the smoke, 'drinking it' with evident delight. They called the reed 'tobacco', hence the common name of the plant. The natives in America had discovered that smoking tobacco relieved thirst and hunger and gave them pleasure in their hard living conditions. It was especially useful during their long trips through the hot and desolate desert regions. As there was no water and food was scarce, smoking tobacco, or chewing it, helped them to survive. The effect must have been similar to the use of coca leaves in the Andes.

People were also aware of the plant's highly toxic effect. They used it as a weapon against deadly snakes. A bunch of loose tobacco leaves would be thrown at the snake and when the leaves touched its skin, the reaction to the poison was very fast. The snake became partly intoxicated and lost its momentum. Then using a long stick, more tobacco was quickly put into the snake's open mouth. As a result, the deadly snake lost its senses and could be killed easily.

The effects of the tobacco plant were also exploited for other purposes. Indian shamans had a custom of hard smoking—they smoked many pipes one after another without a break. As a result of strong intoxication they experienced a kind of trance during which they divined the future.

In ancient Mexico priests were also familiar with the power of tobacco to change perceptions of reality. Instead of smoking they preferred to use a tobacco ointment. Under the ointment's influence their behaviour changed dramatically. Priests were able to kill a human and remove his heart in sacrificial ceremonies without fear or distress and then could go alone to remote woods at night without being afraid.

The custom of smoking tobacco was unknown in Europe until the sixteenth century, when it was brought from America. Ironically, it was pirates who first brought tobacco back from their 'criminal' voyages to the New World. At first tobacco smoking was the privilege of the aristocracy but soon the custom spread to all European countries and reached all classes. It became so prevalent in Italy that Pope Urban VIII issued a special decree to suppress the dangerous 'stinking habit'. Similarly, King James I of England, in 1603 issued a special pamphlet known as 'A Counterblaste to Tobacco' in which he officially condemned the habit of smoking tobacco. The Sultan of Turkey declared cigarette smoking a serious crime and prohibited its use, while the Russian Tsar Michael Romanov made smoking such a serious offence, that those found using tobacco would have their noses cut off.

Queen Catherine de Medici was the first to find that by simply sniffing powdered tobacco leaves, she was able to relieve migraine. Soon, other members of the aristocracy followed her example and the new custom of tobacco sniffing developed. This time the plant became known as the queen's herb and the miraculous healing power was attributed to tobacco.

During the great plague of London in 1665 tobacco was considered the best antidote and preventative measure. Everybody tried to get tobacco and smoke it all day. Even small children were encouraged by their parents to have a smoke, so they smoked a pipe day and night in the belief that it would dispel the disease.

The custom of tobacco smoking reached Africa and became a popular pastime among many African tribes. The heaviest smokers were the Kawarondo tribe in Africa. There, men could be seen smoking not just one but four cigarettes simultaneously, a cigarette in each nostril and the other two in each side of the mouth. A peculiar way to smoke indeed.

An example of how poisonous tobacco leaves are is the story of a smuggler who strapped tobacco leaves to his belly to bring the prohibited stuff over a border. He was found dead on the other side of the border. The contact of the leaves with his skin was sufficient to kill the man on his journey.

Despite all the interesting and often amusing stories about tobacco, one thing remains certain—using tobacco on an everyday basis is very risky indeed. Tobacco is among the most powerful poisons known and its liquid alkaloid, nicotine, is one of the deadliest poisons known. Some people who are involved in fighting the dangerous habit of cigarette smoking call its use a 'long-term suicide' and that is not an exaggeration. Scientifically based evidence leaves no doubt about the danger. There is a much higher incidence of lung cancer, heart disease and other serious illnesses among habitual users of tobacco. And habitual use during pregnancy is regarded as hazardous to the unborn child. It is probably worth knowing that some five hundred people in Australia each year have to have their legs amputated as a result of the destructive effects of tobacco smoking on their blood vessels. This figure should frighten those who have not yet quit the dangerous habit, and those who intend to try tobacco just for fun.

Dangerous Beauty

A handsome lily (*Gloriosa superba*) grows in tropical regions of Africa. Its flowers have a unique appearance. The bright red petals are short and very narrow, and they are bent back, exposing showy large stamens more distinct than the corolla itself. The plant is a real beauty among lilies and it is little wonder that it is called the glory lily.

It is hard to believe that this beautiful plant is among the most dangerous plants of the tropics. All parts, especially the roots, are deadly poisons when eaten. Natives in Africa are aware of the properties of this plant and avoid it, but still in some parts of the tropics it has been used as medicine and a herb to induce abortion. In some regions glory lily is grown in gardens as an ornamental. Cases of severe poisoning have occurred with this plant and sometimes the roots are used as a poison to get rid of enemies. A case was reported in Sri Lanka in which a woman drank a decoction of the roots of the glory lily by mistake. She lost consciousness and was critically ill but recovered after hospital treatment. After the poisoning the woman's hair fell out and after some twenty days she was completely bald as a result of the unusual action of the poison. Fortunately the hair started to regrow and she recovered after about two months.

Children are particularly vulnerable to this plant's poisoning effects and care should be exercised to prevent small children from chewing its flowers or other parts when the glory lily is grown at home.

In some parts of Africa the plant is used to commit suicide and is often called the 'plant for suicide'.

5.

Insidious Plants

Stinger Tree

Some plants are dangerous to touch. The most dreadful among them is the stinger tree (*Dendrocnide moroides*), native to Australia. This tree grows up to 30 m tall in the rainforests of Queensland. The plants are most dangerous when still in the form of a shrub or low tree, as their leaves are most easily brushed against at low level. The effect of direct contact with this leaf is most unpleasant. A field scientist had the following experience:

> I started worming my way through the big green stem, but soon cravenly turned back. The edge of a leaf, camouflaged in the speckled shadow, had stroked my bare forearms . . . As a measure of the sensitivity of the stinging tree I state . . . for the rest of the day and part of the next my arm was so painful, at first very painful indeed. The sting then degenerated into a tingling itch. This I felt for a fortnight. Moreover, fully three months later the tingle returned whenever I bathed my arm in cold water.

In another case, a man fell over the foliage of a freshly cut stinger tree after bathing naked in a jungle pool and experienced such unbearable pain that he was unable to walk or even get up. It took two strong men to carry him to a doctor who had to use morphine injections to relieve the intense suffering. In this case a very large area of skin was affected, hence such severe irritation.

Stinger trees are hated by forest workers, who have to use gloves to prevent hazardous contact with the tree. Not only the fresh leaves are dangerous. Dried leaves, after falling to the ground form a dust which has a strong irritating power. It can cause unpleasant and prolonged sneezing. One scientist who studied bats in the forests of Queensland said: 'I gasped like a machine. I sneezed while I checked the species in the camp. I sneezed as I walked around about to assess its size, and I went on sneezing for an hour or more after we left the scrub'. Woodcutters are aware of the danger of the dust and take necessary precautions. A bushwalker was frightened once when he suddenly saw a group of people wearing masks. He thought that a chemical war had broken out in Australia.

The stinger tree caused a lot of trouble to early European settlers. When they explored the virgin forest in Queensland their horses, irritated by the stinging foliage, often bolted, inflicting bad injuries. Even now some animals are badly injured as a result of contact with the stingers. Dogs are especially vulnerable. They try to stop the severe itching and often bite off the afflicted area of skin. As a result the animal may cause deep wounds and severe bleeding.

The unusual reaction is caused by the stinging hairs covering the surface of the leaves. Each hair has a glass-like bulb, containing an irritating liquid. The hair is as sharp as a needle and breaks easily, injecting the fluid into the skin like a tiny syringe. As the leaf is covered by hundreds of such needles, little wonder that the effect of so many is severe. In the past locals applied an adhesive plaster to the affected area of the skin. When the plaster was removed it also removed parts of the broken ends of the leaf hairs and hence reduced the severity of the sting. Nowadays some anti-allergic medicines are used to relieve the symptoms of irritation.

There are several other stinger plants in Australia, but these seem to cause a less severe sting.

Similar effects are caused by other unrelated plants which are native to East Africa. There is a tree-like herb (*Obetia pinnatifida*) common in some parts of Kenya. Not only the leaves but also the stems of this plant are dangerous to touch. It is covered with whitish, irritating hairs, but their sting is not as strong as that of the Australian plant. The authors experienced this plant's sting when studying the composition of the irritating liquid of the tiny hairs. The itch is most unpleasant, but completely disappears after one hour. This unusual itching property is well known to natives of Africa. It is even utilised in a peculiar way. After the corn harvest is completed, branches of obetia plant are placed closely around the corn store. Rodents quickly learn to avoid the store.

Evil Plant

There is a small tree (*Grevillea mimosoides*), native to Australia, which bears fruits that are even dangerous to touch. The first white explorers who were not aware of this had most unpleasant experiences. During Ludwig Leichhardt's famous expedition (1845) in the uncharted forests of north Queensland, one of the members of the expedition was severely burned. It was a young boy named John Murphy who was searching for unknown fruits in the new region. He gathered a few pods of this plant and, having no pockets, he simply placed the pods inside his shirt. Initially there was no problem at all, but after a few hours when they had returned to their camp, the boy suddenly felt a burning sensation on the belly region where he had kept the fruits. He discovered with horror that his skin was covered with large, black watery blisters. These caused excruciating, burning pain, as if the skin had been drenched with caustic soda.

The fruits, or pods are about 2.5 cm long and are covered with a sticky brown liquid which is a strong skin irritant. Australian Aborigines are aware of the danger; they never rest in the shade of these trees as the sticky drops may fall and cause irritation.

Even some animals have experienced the unpleasant nature of this plant. It has been observed that cockatoos, although fond of fruit, never prey on this plant.

Other plants which are dangerous to touch are poison ivy (*Rhus toxicodendron*), and sumach (*Rhus succedanea*), which was occasionally cultivated in southern Australia. Contact with these plants causes severe skin irritation. Children who climb the sumach tree develop severe dermatitis on the legs, arms and face. In some botanic gardens in Europe, this plant is surrounded by a fence and carries a sign warning people not to touch it.

This tree is now declared a dangerous plant in South Australia and illustrated posters are distributed in most libraries to warn people.

Dangerous Spurges

An interesting euphorbia which is native to South Africa is *Euphorbia ingens*, a tree-like plant up to 9 m in height. This plant is very attractive because its branches form a huge candelabra and it is known as the candelabra tree. It is often planted in African villages as an ornamental plant, and in some parts of East Africa it is so common that it has become known as a characteristic plant of the African savannah. The plant is dangerous to touch because it has sharp, long spines which can cause severe injury. In addition the plant exudes a milky sap, which is injurious to the skin and eyes.

In South Africa candelabra trees are often grown near huts to ward off evil spirits. In some regions it is the custom, when twins are born, for the father of the children to immediately plant two candelabra trees one beside the other just in front of the hut so that the miraculous plant will ward off evil and the children will grow up unharmed. Nobody risks cutting down these trees, even if the hut has already been destroyed and the people who lived there have died. Two proud candelabra trees still guard the place where the twins were born long ago.

Candelabra trees are favoured by those in power. One Zulu chief ordered his throne to be erected beneath the largest candelabra found in the area.

Some euphorbia plants, with their dangerous spines, are often used in Africa to make hedges to restrain livestock. But a strongly spined *Euphorbia desmondii*, native to Africa, is occasionally grown for another purpose. It was used in the past, particularly in Nigeria, as a natural 'wall' to deter hostile neighbours. The thorny spurge, when planted around the whole village made an almost impenetrable fence, which no one would dare penetrate. Those who tried to cut their way through were not only severely scratched by the heavy spines, but were also blinded by the highly irritating sap which exuded from the branches. A fast growing spurge hedge became an almost ideal line of defence.

Dangerous Finger Cherry

Australia is the home of some most unusual plants, but one really frightened people, especially in the early 1920s, when it was found that its fruits can cause permanent blindness. The fruits of a small tree *Rhodomyrtus macrocarpa*, Finger Cherry, native to northern Queensland, were pleasant to taste, and were often consumed in large quantities, especially by children. No-one expected danger. But, soon cases of temporary and even permanent blindness were reported, and they were always associated with eating these fruit. The situation was so serious that in 1920 the Queensland government declared an alert and to prevent poisoning, special illustrated posters were distributed to schools. Lectures were organised to explain the danger and to help with the recognition by children of the hazardous tree.

One elderly man's long term blindness was investigated in 1944 by doctors. In his early childhood he was living in Queensland and went blind after eating large amounts of a tasty fruit. Being the eldest of the group of children he was the one who climbed the tree, so he had a chance to help himself to the ripest and the best, while he threw down the unripe and green ones to other children waiting below. While the rest of the children had no problems, he went blind. The man was found to have had his optic nerve irreversibly damaged.

Cases of blindness as a result of eating the fruit were rare but usually occurred among Aborigines who ate them.

The tree is also found in the forests of Papua New Guinea. In 1945, there was a report in the *Courier-Mail* of a horrible mass-poisoning among soldiers who consumed the fruits of this plant. Twenty-seven soldiers went blind, but the report does not specify what quantity of fruit had been consumed.

It still remains unclear why the fruit causes such a terrible effect. Some authors claim that only ripe fruits are dangerous, others say that it is the green and unripe fruit which are the most hazardous. Some even suggest that the optic nerve-damaging substance is not in the fruit itself but is a highly poisonous fungus infesting the fruit. What all scientists are certain of is that all those who went blind had consumed very large quantities of the fruit in one sitting.

The dangerous fruits are fleshy, cylindrical and up to 2.5 cm long. They are green at first, and as they ripen, change to bright red and finally become deep red. Each fruit has five persistent sepals of the calyx at the tip. The fruit contains kidney-shaped seeds about 8 mm in diameter.

As the fruits may resemble known edible fruits there is always a potential danger of eating them by mistake. With the increasing number of people going into the forests where this plant grows it is essential that people are instructed not to consume fruits even if they are tasty.

6.

Mysterious Mushrooms

Lady in the Veil

There are many mushrooms whose fruiting bodies are a peculiar shape, but the most extraordinary is, no doubt, *Dictyophora phalloides*, native to Australia and Africa. This mushroom which grows in tropical forests has an astonishing shape with a striking resemblance to a human penis. But this is just the first of the surprises which this fungus has for those who have the opportunity to observe its miraculous development. Once it has grown to its full height, a white, very delicate membrane, forms beneath the cap like an attractive lady's dress. Little wonder that the first botanists called this mushroom 'Lady in the Veil'. Some have even called it 'flowering fungus' as it resembles the attractive white corolla of a mysterious flower rather than a mushroom.

The remarkable spectacle offered by the fungus does not last long, and soon the attractive lady becomes more eccentric. From its delicate veil a sticky mucilaginous fluid starts to exude, and produces a disgusting smell like rotting flesh. This surprising change destroys the whole spectacle; its striking appearance is not designed to attract people but to lure carrion flies who are now attracted even more by the stench. Crawling on the sticky fluid, which contains thousands of spores, the insects swallow the food prepared by the clever plant. And, flying away, the insects distribute fungus spores in their faeces. In this way the Lady in the Veil has assured the survival of the species.

It is interesting that this fungus has another unique characteristic and that is it grows extremely fast. It takes only twenty minutes to grow from a small, egg-like fruiting body to a peculiar 'stock', some 20 cm in height, which then develops its full dress. During this unusually rapid growth the expanding cells make a clearly audible peculiar cracking sound. This fungus is among the fastest growing organisms in the plant kingdom.

Luminescent Fungi

People in ancient times were amazed when they saw that certain trees glowed in the dark but were not burning. When this was seen in a cemetery, people were frightened, believing they saw ghosts of the dead.

Luminosity is caused by fungi, mycelia, which penetrate the dead wood of some species of old trees. Pieces of such wood were used in the past in Scandinavia as lanterns to illuminate people's paths in the

Candelabra tree
Euphorbia ingens
(see Insidious Plants,
pg. 54)

Lady in the veil
Dictyophora sp.

dark. Using the wood, they could safely go into barns filled with hay without danger of causing a fire.

In the past the glowing root was regarded as magical and possession of one was thought to give the owner the power to change any metal into gold.

The unusual property of pieces of old wood to glow at night was well known to soldiers during the First World War. It was customary to wear luminescent wood pieces on helmets or on rifles to avoid collision in the trenches at night when fire or other illumination was a great risk.

Even during the Second World War, paratroopers in the occupied territory in France, were once greatly frightened when they saw a number of small shining objects lying in the fields. We can imagine how relieved they were when they later saw the innocent pieces of wood and realised what had caused such alarm.

Old timbers used in mines as support often shine luminously in complete darkness underground. One miner reported: 'I saw the luminous plants here in wonderful beauty. It appeared, on descending into the mine, as if we were entering an enchanted castle . . . the roofs and walls and pillars were entirely covered with them, and the beautiful light they cast around almost dazzled the eye. The light they gave out is like faint moonshine, so that two persons near each other could readily distinguish their bodies'.

The wood of old trees is not the only thing attacked by luminescent fungi. The fruiting bodies of certain mushrooms are also known to exhibit the same phenomenon, but with even greater strength. In Indonesia such fungi are common in tropical forests. They are collected by girls who adorn their heads with pieces of the mushroom, 'to guide their lovers when walking at night in the bush'.

An American correspondent gave an amazing report in his letter home from New Guinea during the Second World War: 'Darling, I am writing to you tonight by the light of five mushrooms'. A similar experience with fluorescent mushrooms was described by Henry Drummond, a British explorer who penetrated the region of Swan Valley in Australia. He collected an unusually large specimen of *Agaricus* species, weighing some 2.5 kg, and brought it to his hut where he hung it beside the fireplace. When he returned from a night walk he saw his whole room illuminated with an unusual light. He learned with surprise that it was his huge mushroom which was responsible. He said that the huge fungus kept shining for about five nights until the mushroom dried completely and its luminescence ceased.

Some mushrooms are known for the strength of their luminescence. For example, the fruiting body of *Mycena lux-coeli*, native to Hachijo Island of Japan, can be seen in the dark from about 15 m. From a distance, these mushrooms clustered together look like small lanterns.

It is still not clear why some fungi emit light. Some authors suggest that the plants shine to attract certain insects which will assist in the dispersal of spores. The most common luminescent mushrooms belong to the genus *Agaricus*.

Vegetable Caterpillar

In medieval times people were puzzled by strange creatures, half animal and half plant, when they discovered that a club outgrowth forming on the dead body of a larvae was a fungus. They called these unusual creatures vegetable caterpillars and believed that they exemplified a transmutation from the plant to the animal kingdom. As often happens with such unusual objects, a remarkable healing power was attributed to them. These objects have been collected, especially in Tibet, and then sold to the Chinese who used them as a popular tonic and rejuvenating medicine. Oriental shops still offer dried vegetable caterpillars as a folk medicine to cure various ailments.

It was not until the early nineteenth century that the true nature of such objects was recognised. We now know that it is the result of the fungus (*Cordyceps* species) attacking the larvae of certain insects which live underground. The caterpillar becomes infected with the sticky spores of the fungus. Once the spores develop on the larvae's surface, the mycelia proceed to penetrate the inner tissue of the larvae. The fungus gradually replaces the whole inner tissue of the larvae, leaving only the skin intact.

Soon the fungus develops a long stalk which pierces the host's skin and grows upwards, to reach the soil surface. It is therefore a fungus arising from a completely destroyed larval body which is known as vegetable caterpillar.

Most fungal outgrowths are some 5-7 cm long, but those of an Australian *Cordyceps gardneri*, can be 30 cm long. The size of the fungus outgrowth depends on how deep in the soil the larvae was when it was attacked. The deeper the soil the longer the parasitic fungus. Parasitic fungi usually attack the larvae of such insects as moths and cockroaches. Some may even attack other fungi. But they usually attack the soft bodies of larvae.

A fungus, *Cordyceps sphecocephala*, native to the West Indies, has another habit. It attacks certain adult insects. Long antler-like outgrowths on the insects make them strange objects indeed. The flying capacity of an insect who may live for some time, is greatly disturbed. Finally the parasitic fungus will completely 'eat' its host from the inside.

Gigantic Mushroom

Some mushrooms when mature resemble a large ball rather than a fungus. They are commonly called puffballs and they are easy to distinguish because of their snow-white colour when young. These fungi can grow to an incredible size and weight. One specimen, *Calvatia gigantea*, found in the USA was 155 cm in circumference, which makes it the world's largest known fungus. Normally puffballs are some 20-30 cm across.

When the puffball is mature the touch of a falling twig or an animal paw, causes the brittle cover of the sac to break and the fungus explodes, releasing its contents in the form of a brownish cloud. This cloud is composed of an incalculable number of minute spores. An average sized puffball may contain 1,000,000,000,000, (one trillion) spores, a number impossible to imagine. It has been estimated that if every spore germinated and produced a new fungus, the resulting fungi could form a five-fold ring around the globe.

Fortunately not many spores survive. Although they are easily carried by the wind and can cover enormous distances, many land on water or in the desert and most spores perish. It is incredible how far these tiny spores can travel with the air currents. It has been estimated that they can be carried for nearly half a million kilometres. Tiny puffball spores have been detected in the air up to 10 km above sea level.

Puffballs are not just a botanical curiosity. When immature their flesh is white and edible. One large mushroom was found to be a life saver for a whole family during an emergency.

When the puffball is mature and full of spores, the spores can be collected and used to stop bleeding as they are very absorbent. In the past puffballs were commonly used to stop the bleeding of men wounded in battle.

The spores of puffballs of the *Lycoperdon* species have been used in Mexico in the past in magic rituals. When eaten they are supposed to enhance a kind of mind-altering effect. In some regions the spores of certain puffballs have been used as a medicine to induce sleep.

Shameless Mushrooms

Some mushrooms have a bad reputation just because of their peculiar appearance. Such are the various members of the genus *Phallus*, which both in shape and colour strikingly resemble a human penis. Little wonder that *Phallus impudicus*, a mushroom common in Europe, literally means 'shameless penis'. Such mushrooms are also known for their nauseatingly unpleasant odour when ripe. So in the Middle Ages people regarded these 'creatures' as a manifestation of the Devil. It was believed that touching such a mushroom could cause a dreadful disease.

These phallic fungi were regarded as obscene objects, to be avoided even to the extent of not looking in their direction. But the biggest enemy

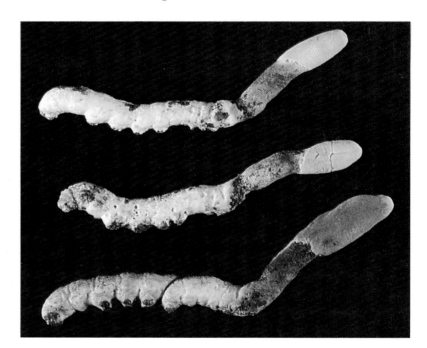

Caterpillar fungus
Cordyceps hawksii

Stinkhorn
Phallus rubicundus

of indecent mushrooms was an eccentric English lady, known as Aunt Etty, who during the reign of Queen Victoria, took it upon herself 'to protect the morals of our maidens'. Every day she walked around in the woods, wearing gloves, and gathered 'shameless' mushrooms and destroyed them.

These indecent plants, called stink-horns, were a cause of many incidents in the past. In 1926, in France, an abbot was severely beaten by the adherents of a certain religious sect called 'Our Lady of Tears', as a result of a very unusual accusation. The abbot was thought to have sent a flock of demonic birds to the gardens of the sect. A great number of the most obscene mushrooms appeared from the birds' droppings. The sect said that the 'fungi of obscene shapes . . . emitted such appalling odours that those who inhaled them were smitten by horrendous disease.'

Phallic fungi are common in the forests of Papua New Guinea, where they appear in masses after heavy rain. The natives watch these mushrooms growing with awe. They often sit and observe the strange transformation of a tiny egg-like fungus into a powerful smelling phallus-like structure. The whole process of expansion is quite rapid, often being completed in 1½ hours.

Many stink-horns are edible when young, and they are often collected and sold at the local markets. But when the phalloid-type mushroom is mature, its 'head' is covered with slime, and gives off the smell of rotten flesh, to lure flies. Crawling on this 'juicy' surface the flies consume the juice together with the tiny spores and then distribute them with their faeces.

Calluses of the Soil

The edible mushrooms we know are usually an attractive colour or shape, and grow above the soil. Collection of such mushrooms is a pleasant pastime in many regions. But certain fungi, called Truffles (*Tuber* species) grow underground. These mushrooms are rather unattractive, irregular shaped objects which may be likened more to a stone or potato tuber than to a mushroom. It is little wonder that such objects found under the soil puzzled naturalists who initially regarded them as calluses of the soil, or an evil soil formation. Some considered them to occur as a result of the combined action of thunder, rain and the rays of the sun on the soil.

The origin of truffles remained a mystery for many centuries. Even in the sixteenth century truffles were still believed to be a peculiar product of deer semen. As the peculiar objects were mostly found in the ground beneath certain trees such as oaks in Europe, their origin was associated with the roots of the tree. Since flies were often seen in swarms above where truffles grew, another theory was introduced that the female fly lays an egg inside the small roots of the oak to produce the gall-like outgrowths.

We know now that truffles are sometimes attacked by certain fly larvae and when the fungus is ripe, swarms of little flies may be seen above the spot where the truffles are buried. This was the reason for the peculiar theory of a relation between the flies and the strange fungi.

It is true that truffles emit a smell which is pleasant to some but disgusting to others. Some people find the odour resembles rancid bacon. Some even say that it is like 'sewer gas'. But most people seem to like the flavour as truffles are considered to be among the most delicious of mushrooms and their excellent and unique taste makes them the most expensive food and delicacy in many regions.

Our sense of smell is too weak to detect a truffle underground, so certain animals with an excellent 'nose' are always used for truffle hunting. In France they use specially trained pigs, especially a pregnant sow, which is known for its unique sense of smell. Such hunting looks quite peculiar. The farmer usually carries his animal in a wheelbarrow so that it does not tire itself before hunting. Once in the woods, the farmer puts a lead around the pig's neck and hunting commences. As soon as the animal finds a truffle, she starts to root it out, making a hole. At this moment the farmer quickly takes the pig away, and digs up the truffle himself. Otherwise the pig would eat the delicious mushroom herself.

Pigs are known to be able to smell a truffle up to 70 m away. In Italy, trained dogs are mainly used for truffle hunting. In the past even specially trained bears were occasionally used for truffle hunting.

Australian Aborigines can detect the presence of truffles under the earth without the assistance of dogs. They simply look for a hairline crack in the sand and dig the mushrooms up, using wooden sticks. The most common is the so-called native truffle (*Elderia arenivaga*) which is collected and eaten by Aborigines in desert areas.

It is interesting that Australia is the home of a mushroom which resembles a truffle as it lives underground but is not a true truffle. Called a native bread (*Polyporus mylittae*) this mushroom, when dug up, is often mistaken for a large stone—hence its popular name, 'stone fungus'. It is a giant among mushrooms as some specimens reach an incredible weight of 20 kg. The mushroom's white flesh is roasted on a fire and then eaten by the Aborigines. Its taste is not very good but the Aborigines regard it as a delicacy and it became known as blackfellow's bread. These giant underground fungi may be 30 cm in diameter.

7.
Giants of the Plant Kingdom

Vegetable Monster

Among the strange plants in the world the most peculiar is certainly the baobab tree (*Adansonia digitata*). Michael Adanson, who discovered this unique tree in Senegal in 1794, reported 'I perceived a tree of a prodigious thickness. I do not believe the like was ever seen in any part of the world'. The tree is really incredible with its obese trunk some 9 m in diameter. It is in fact one of the thickest plants known, exceeded only by the American sequoias. It is rather a short tree, and this is the reason why when seen without leaves it may be likened to a prehistoric fossil. Early explorers called the tree vegetable dinosaur or even vegetable monster, it was so unusual. When the obese tree is leafless, during the dry season, it looks like a huge carrot growing upside down.

Baobabs are very common plants in the savannahs of East Africa, especially in Kenya and Tanzania. Thousands of magnificent baobabs can be seen on both sides of the road from Nairobi to Mombasa as baobabs are the dominant species of the whole landscape, and are most impressive for those coming to Africa for the first time. But many if not all the trees are partly damaged. It is elephants which are to blame, as they relish the soft wood of the baobab, and have such an appetite that they can almost completely consume this huge tree. As they can easily pierce the trunk, elephants also drink the water accumulated in the hollow trees. In the Tsavo National Park elephants are occasionally found dead beneath a fallen giant baobab trunk. Africans remark that at least sometimes the tree can take its revenge.

Old baobabs are often hollow and fill with water during the rainy season to become a natural well for thirsty travellers. So the baobab tree can be a life saver as well.

Hollow baobabs are also used in Africa as temporary shelters or even bars to sell a locally made beer. A rather peculiar and amusing use has been found for one hollow tree. It was equipped with flushing water and for a long time, it was said, served as a luxury toilet.

In some areas of Africa hollow baobabs were used in an entirely different way. The bodies of those who had broken tribal laws or victims who did not deserve a decent burial, were simply hanged inside the tree. The body was usually preserved and mummified well in the hot and dry conditions.

As if everything should be extraordinary about this tree, its flowers are also unique. One flower may contain an enormous number of stamens,

African baobab
Adansonia digitata

Bamboo, the giant grass

Traveller's tree
*Ravenala
madagascariensis*

up to 2000. The flowers are showy and fleshy. They are believed to be inhabited by spirits. In some areas it is believed that anyone who picks a baobab flower will be killed by a lion.

The fruits resemble cucumbers and they hang on long rope-like peduncles. They contain a sour flesh from which a refreshing drink is prepared. The fruits are often collected in Africa by baboons who relish their flesh, hence another name—monkey bread tree.

The baobab tree is not only found in Africa—related plants are also native to Madagascar and Australia. In these countries it is also among the thickest trees known. Called the boab in Australia, it was discovered in 1856 by the explorer Gregory and therefore the plant was named *Adansonia gregorii*. He saw this peculiar, obese tree up to 6 m in diameter on the bank of the Victoria River. On the trunk of one baobab he carved a short message to another explorer; it became famous as the 'letter in the oven' which is a reference to the hot conditions in the area. It is still legible over 130 years later. Members of his expedition learnt from the Aborigines how to use the boab's fruit. Gregory reported: 'We boiled the interior substance of the baobab fruits with sugar and found it to be of material assistance to their rapid recovery.' They were suffering from severe scurvy and it was baobab with its vitamin C in abundance which rescued the travellers.

Among the peculiar uses of this tree in Australia, one deserves to be mentioned. An old and hollow baobab which grows some miles from Wyndham in the valley of the King River, used to be used as a prison for cattle thieves. It was said to readily accommodate 18 prisoners at a time. But even more famous is another tree growing near Derby in the Northern Territory, which has become famous as a prison tree. This hollow trunk has a special doorway in one side, and two holes on the tree top provide fresh air. Ironically this prison has never been used for its purpose. Despite this it is still a great tourist attraction. The residents of Derby are proud of their baobab and an annual celebration known as the boab festival, is held in the shade of the famous 'prison tree'.

Mammoth Tree   Among the most impressive trees in the world are the famous evergreen sequoias (*Sequoia sempervirens*) native to California. These are the world's tallest trees as they reach a remarkable height of over 100 m. The highest, and still living sequoia, known as the 'tallest tree' measures exactly 110.3 m, and this is the world record. Because of the trees' red colour, these magnificent plants are called redwoods. Protection of this unique tree became a national priority, and today it grows in twenty Redwood State Parks, of which the most important is the Sequoia National Park.

Sequoia used to be regarded as an important timber and many

giant trees have been lost. On the stump of one giant sequoia it was said, 'a piano, and four members of the band were placed and there was enough space for fourteen pairs to dance freely'. The stump must have been very wide indeed but no exact diameter was indicated. According to another report, the timber obtained from one sequoia tree was so huge that thirty huge railway trucks had to be used to bring the timber to the sawmill.

Another remarkable American tree, which competes with the sequoia in height, but beats it in its enormous thickness, is the *Sequoiadendron giganteum*, known as the mammoth tree. Although the tallest mammoth is 'only' 92 m high, it may attain a thickness of more than 10 m. So the mammoth trees are among the thickest trees in the world. The thickest ever measured, which no longer exists, was said to have an incredible diameter of 14.45 m. But the thickest mammoth tree still living is 'General Grant' which is 92 m high, and its diameter immediately above the ground is 12.5 m, a remarkable giant indeed. There were reports in the past of one mammoth tree, called, 'Father of the Forest', which was 125 m high. But there is no real proof that this was a correct measurement.

Mammoth trees are now also under protection and the most important is in the Yosemite National Park.

These living monuments of nature are also among the oldest trees in the world, and some are estimated to be 4000 years old. Sequoias are covered with a thick bark which has served as an excellent protection against fire. It is spongy and tough and almost fireproof, and it is up to 60 cm thick.

Australian Giants

Eucalypts, commonly known as gum trees (*Eucalyptus* species) were once considered to be the tallest trees in the world. Some early naturalists reported huge gum trees which they claimed were 150 m high, but such reports were never confirmed. In 1888, at the Centennial exhibition in Melbourne, a huge gum tree trunk was exhibited and the label attached to it claimed that it was cut from a 120 m tall tree. But again there was no way to prove it. A special prize was offered to anyone who could find a gum tree over 120 m tall, but the prize was never claimed. The tallest properly measured eucalypt was Tasmanian, *Eucalyptus regnans* called the mountain ash. It reached a remarkable height of 107 m. Unfortunately this specimen does not exist any more. The highest living tree is still a *E. regnans*, found in the Styx Valley in Tasmania which measures exactly 99 m. Australians are proud of this tree and say that it was the highest tree in the world apart from coniferous plants. But this remarkable gum tree is exceeded by the American sequoia.

Eucalypts are among the most important timber trees in the world and they have been cultivated around the world, often with Australia's assistance, as for example in China. But the first country to which this tree was introduced was Ethiopia. In 1888 the Emperor Menelik II brought eucalypts from Australia to decorate his new established capital Addis Ababa. Even the name of the capital, which literally means 'new flower', refers to the attractive eucalypts decorating this African city.

The gum tree is one of the fastest growing trees, and is also known to take enormous amounts of water from the soil. This characteristic was exploited in Italy. To eradicate marshes near Rome, eucalypts were planted, and where other measures had failed in the past, the Australian tree was successful. Malaria was eradicated as the mosquitos carrying this deadly disease lost their habitat.

Some eucalypts produce an enormous number of fragrant flowers. One tree (*Eucalyptus intermedia*) has flowers which are full of honey-like nectar. These flowers are collected by the Aborigines. They steep the fragrant flowers in water and use it as a refreshing drink.

The most wicked use of eucalypts is that of young Aborigines who have found that certain birds such as parakeets are particularly fond of the nectar of some eucalypt flowers. They have noticed that the parent birds collect the nectar which is then fed to their offspring in the nest. So, observant boys spend much time searching for these nests. They climb up the tree, and collect the young birds which have just been fed. Holding a bird upside down, and putting its beak into the mouth, causes the tiny bird to disgorge the sweet contents of its stomach. This peculiar custom was first reported in 1881.

Eucalypts have an interesting relationship with the koala. This magnificent marsupial, the favourite 'teddy-bear', which has become a symbol of Australian wildlife, could perish as its life depends on gum trees. Their only food is that of eucalypt leaves, and the animal dies if the one particular species out of 500 it chooses is not available. Koalas can only live on a few gum trees, and the animal easily recognises the right one. They have a specially adapted digestive system for this unusual diet: with the leaves the koala consumes a considerable quantity of fragrant volatile oil which would certainly kill other animals. The koala has such a great appetite that living on one tree it can completely defoliate the canopy and cause the host tree to die.

The massive destruction of eucalypt forests in Australia, has endangered those gum tree species on which the life of the koala depends. Fortunately special sanctuaries have been established where this remarkable animal can safely live and be observed by enthusiasts.

Banyan
Ficus benghalensis

Giant Grass

Among the largest and fastest growing grasses in the whole plant kingdom are bamboos. The tallest are *Dendrocalamus giganteus*, native to Burma, and called giant bamboos. They may occasionally reach the remarkable height of 40 m. Astonishingly the hollow stem of this plant does not exceed 30 cm in diameter at the base.

Bamboo grows exceedingly fast and its stem may increase up to one metre in 24 hours. The growth of a young shoot is so vigorous at its early stage that the bamboo shoot, when piercing its way through the culm-covering sheet, may produce a distinct noise. One Chinaman described hearing this during his travels through a region where bamboos were growing wild. 'Before the dawn he was awakened by an awful squeaking, whining, and faint screaming coming from the bamboo grove, he called his companion, who explained to him that the noises were produced by the growth of the shoots of young giant bamboos . . . as they pierced their way through the bracts and sheets clothing the base of each shoot'.

The incredibly fast elongation of the bamboo culm was used by the ancient Chinese for the punishment of criminals. In this most cruel method a convicted man was strongly fastened to the growing bamboo culms and left alone in the forest. The fast growing plant inflicted death in great agony by stretching the body.

It is interesting to note that this giant grass has an unusual characteristic, in that despite its long life, the plants of the same species all die together once they bear flowers and produce seeds. Some flower and die after 33 years, others after exactly 66 and some even after 100 years. As bamboo plants bloom so rarely, anyone in Asia who is known to have witnessed two bamboo flowering periods is regarded as a very old person. A mass flowering of the *Phyllostachys bambusoides* bamboo occurred in 1987 in Japan, and it was exactly 100 years since this plant had flowered last.

When all the plants died after flowering, the Japanese used to say that the bamboo had committed mass suicide and were greatly concerned. Little wonder, as bamboos are extremely useful plants and the simultaneous death of all the plantations causes great economic loss.

In East Africa, sudden mass flowering of bamboo forests is seen as an omen, as the death of the plant may be a sign of a calamity to come. Indeed, in 1980, after a mass flowering of bamboo in Kenya in areas near Nairobi, a bubonic plague epidemic broke out which killed many people. The massive amount of grain produced by the bamboo after flowering led to a dramatic increase of the rat population which are the hosts of the fleas that transfer the deadly disease. In this unusual way the magnificent bamboo plant may be the source of a deadly plague.

Bamboo is an extremely useful plant, and is used for a wide variety of purposes from timber for furniture making, to bridges, sewerage and even musical instruments. Small wonder that the Chinese poet Pou-Son-

Tung wrote some 800 years ago: 'A meal should have meat, but the house must have bamboo'. Many different kinds of bamboo are cultivated with most unusual stem structures. The Japanese have even established a plantation of bamboo with square culms. To do this a square frame was attached around the growing stem. Whenever the apex of a shoot began to show through the top, the frame is moved up to produce a longer square length.

Bamboo has even been used as a poison for criminal purposes. In Africa, the blackish hairs which cover the large bamboo sheets are used. These hairs, which are as sharp as needles, when secretly added to food, cause the gradual formation of ulcers in the stomach, and may lead to death, which is usually attributed to natural causes. This secret poison used to be used in West Africa when a black servant wanted to get rid of a cruel white master.

Devil's Rope

Early explorers of tropical jungles were often severely scratched by the thorns of snake-like climbing plants which made life miserable. Kerner, a famous German explorer and botanist wrote: 'Everything climbs, winds, and twines with everything else, the eye in vain attempts to ascertain which stem, which foliage and which flowers or fruits, belong to which . . . they appear as swaying garlands, or hanging down as ample curtains from branches of the trees. In other places they stretch in luxuriant festoons from bough to bough and from tree to tree'.

An interesting climbing plant found in the forest is a unique palm, known as rotang palm (*Calamus* species). Its stem is about 5 cm thick and flexible, and by using its sharp spines, the palm can climb the tallest trees. When it reaches the top of the tree this unusual palm spreads to another tree top or descends down to the base of the tree where it continues growing, to form, in effect, an entangled mass of rope-like knots. In fact some rotang palms may attain an incredible length of 180 m, a record for the longest plant known.

These palms are hated by those who penetrate the forest as they inflict painful injury when touched. Small wonder that they are often called 'devil's ropes'. Paths through the forest where such palms grow have to be cleared with machetes.

The unpleasant ropes do have one useful quality. The stem, with the spines removed, is almost a ready-made material for furniture. In tropical regions rotang palms are used for many purposes such as building suspension bridges, or as cables for hauling boats or logs. The Australian Aborigines also use rotang palms. They have invented a peculiar method of extracting honey from bee-nests found in hollow trees. From the rotang palm stem they make a kind of brush by fraying its end. This 'device' is then pushed through the hole into the trunk until the rope reaches the nest. By twisting the stem, honey and wax sticks to the brush. This is a clever technique since it does not destroy the nest and the bees cannot sting the intruders.

A similar technique is employed to find eels in submerged hollow logs in which the fish often hide. A rotang rope is poked about in the log under the water and from time to time taken out for inspection. Once a slimy deposit is found on the end of the brush, it is guaranteed that an eel is there to be caught. The Aborigines then dive and catch the fish. In this way, Aborigines avoid wasting time with unnecessary 'fruitless' dives.

Tree with a Thousand Trunks

It is hard to believe that one tree can fill an entire large garden. Such is the case with the famous banyan tree (*Ficus benghalensis*), native to India. When the tree reaches a certain size and its branches are large and thick, it sends down rope-like roots which hang from the branches and elongate. When these roots reach the soil they anchor there, take root and then thicken to form additional pillar-like structures, so that the tree has not one but many trunks. In this unusual way the banyan tree can spread outwards almost indefinitely. After many years of such development one tree is so large and has such a large canopy that it can cover several acres.

In one village in India, a very old banyan has developed 320 additional trunks and covered a large area of some 600 m in circumference. But the most famous Indian banyan is that growing in Calcutta Botanic Gardens. It has over 1700 trunks—a real record in the plant kingdom. The single plant has been growing for some 200 years.

The banyan tree, with its multiple trunks, has been known since antiquity. During Alexander's Indian campaign (327-325 BC), the story says, 20,000 soldiers are said to have taken shelter under one immense banyan tree.

The tree is held in great esteem in India and Buddha is believed to have usually meditated under the shade of a banyan tree. In India, people have special respect for the tree and often help it in its efforts to form new trunks. They cover the hanging root with two halves of a bamboo culm with its end fixed to the ground. They also thoroughly cover the tip of the growing root with moss in order to prevent its damage by rats or squirrels. To help the roots take they also soften the soil.

Traveller's Tree

A most spectacular tropical plant is the traveller's tree (*Ravenala madagascariensis*) which has a unique appearance unlike 'normal' trees. Although it has the usual straight trunk, its leaves are spread vertically so that from afar the tree looks like a gigantic, man-made fan. The formation of this fan is unique as 2 m long stalks carry large banana-like leaves, which are invariably torn into ribbons by the wind. The base of the leafstalks appears from the top of the trunk and forms a type of basket-work. As a result of such an unusual leaf arrangement the tree forms a huge fan, often 30 m tall.

At the base of each leaf stalk there is a kind of cistern. During the rain season water is collected on the ribbed surface of the leaf, and flows down a groove to the 'cistern' where it is stored.

Early travellers noticed that this tree is a source of water in an emergency. In 1859 W. Ellis wrote during his exploration of Madagascar: 'When a spear is stuck into the thick, firm end of the leafstalk, a stream of pure clean water gushes out'. According to some authors, as much as 1½ litres of potable water can be found in one tree, so the tree can be a life saver during the long dry season, hence the name of the plant— the traveller's tree.

The peculiar flat shape of the tree is said to be always directed from north to south, so that the tree can be used as a kind of a compass, especially at night. But according to Menninger, when the plants were grown from seed in a subtropical region, not one of the trees ever pointed north.

In Madagascar where traveller's trees grow in groves, they are known for their resistance to bush fires. Because of this, it grows back quickly and creates secondary forest after fire has destroyed all the other plants in the area.

Because of their spectacular appearance, traveller's trees are often cultivated in tropical regions as ornamentals. This remarkable tree is a distant relative of the banana, although it has a normal woody trunk.

Incredible Ferns

Ferns have always been enjoyed as ornamental plants, and for this reason they are often planted as indoor or garden plants. People from moderate climates are therefore surprised to see tree-like ferns.

Certain ferns such as *Alsophila excelsa*, native to Norfolk Island, may attain the incredible size of 18 m. Such plants, which are in fact large herbaceous plants, are most attractive, and seeing these trees in their natural habitat is an unforgettable experience. Australia is fortunate in this respect and many beautiful tree ferns can be seen, especially in the Gippsland forests in Victoria.

In Kenya, in the Aberdare mountains, magnificent tree ferns grow on the valley sides. These beautiful plants which are usually 3-5 m high are often grown in gardens in various parts of Australia as ornamentals.

However, some ferns native to Australia do not resemble ferns. For example, nardoo plant (*Marsilea drummondii*) is a true fern but its leaves resemble a four-leaved clover. This plant which is only some 20 cm in height, often grows in the arid regions of Australia, and is often found in shallow water. These plants occur in such an abundance in certain areas that they are collected as a food. The ferns produce capsules full of spores, from which a kind of flour can be made. The cake does not taste very nice, but is eaten by the Aborigines in cases of emergency. Nardoo used to be collected in great quantities and was almost a staple food of the Aborigines in Australia in the past. The first Australian explorers occasionally had a chance to try this food. The members of the Burke and Wills expedition in 1861 were reluctant to eat nardoo, a food offered to them by the Aborigines they met. They reported: 'I cannot understand this nardoo at all; it certainly will not agree with me in any form. We are now reduced to it alone, and we manage to get from four to five pounds a day between us'. Unfortunately both men died of starvation, and only one member of the expedition, King, survived. He evidently hated nardoo less and was probably on better terms with the Aborigines he met, as he was able to survive on this unusual diet. Some authors believe that since King shared pituri, he was also provided with some other more nutritious food such as the grubs of certain insects, and this helped him to survive.

It should be mentioned that a common bracken fern (*Pteridium aquilinum*), which has been used as a salad in Australia, Japan and New Zealand, is now regarded as dangerous, because it is known to cause cancer in animals. This plant is often grazed by cows and their milk is therefore not safe to use. The plant has now been recognised as a dangerous weed in Australia, and national programmes have been established to eradicate it. The plant is very difficult to fight. It is the first plant to appear after bush fires. Its spores seem to enjoy heat and they germinate quickly after fire. It is of interest that bracken has been found growing on volcanic lava still hot after eruption, such is the unusual adaptability of this fern.

8.
The Oldest Plants in the World

Incredible Pine

There is a common belief that the taller or thicker the tree, the older it is, but that is not true. It has been discovered that it is not the giant sequoias or the monstrous baobabs, but a humble pine tree which holds the world record for longevity. This is a bristlecone pine (*Pinus aristata*) native to East Nevada in the USA, found to be 4900 years old—an incredible age, if we assume that the pine only grows to some 12 m in height and is of moderate thickness. This remarkable pine is recognised as the oldest living tree, and among the oldest living beings in the world. *

Bristlecone pines grow in small groups on the wind-beaten slopes of mountains, at an elevation of over 3000 m. Where no other plant could survive, this unusual pine can grow for millennia.

These plants are specially adapted to the conditions as the wood is heavily saturated with resin, which is excellent protection against insect attack or decay by fungi. Even those trees which died more than a thousand years ago are still standing as if they were still alive.

The plant holds another record among trees, which is its remarkably slow growth rate. It grows scarcely 0.1 mm in thickness a year, and produces normal annual rings which could be counted as in most other trees. These rings however, are incomparably small and cannot be seen without the aid of a microscope. A study at the University of Arizona revealed that on a piece of wood about 12 cm long cut from an old tree trunk, an incredible 1000 distinct annual rings could be identified.

It is not only the age of the tree which can be determined by the ring countings. In the structure of this unique wood a chronology of certain events, especially climatic changes which took place in the remote past, can be read, as if from a book. Periods of severe drought which took place thousands of years ago can be easily detected, and such study is of great scientific value. Even disasters which occurred not far from the areas where the magnificent old trees grow, can be detected by studying the pieces of wood. For example, the famous earthquake which destroyed San Francisco in 1906 has been recorded in the sensitive wood of the bristlecone pine tree.

*The creosote plant (*Larrea tridentata*) from southwest California was found in 1980 to be 11,700 years old.

Fossil Plants

The cycad (Order *Cycadales*) is the most primitive form of seed-producing plant, and its ancestors were living some 270 million years ago. These magnificent plants, which resemble palms, occur now mainly in Australia and South Africa. They usually produce a thick trunk-like stem from which grow attractive fern-like leaves. These plants give a prehistoric appearance to the places where they grow.

There is one unique feature of the cycads, and that is that they often produce very large cones—in fact the world's largest. One cycad (*Encephalartos caffer*), native to South Africa, produces huge female cones. One, for example, was found to weigh over 45 kg and measure over 60 cm in length. As the cone yields a great number of seeds which are used for food, this cycad became known in South Africa as Hottentot's bread tree.

Cycads produce many seeds, which resemble small plums. Inside the fleshy coat there is a large stone which contains a starchy material. Cycad seeds were often tried as emergency food by explorers when penetrating tropical regions of Australia, Captain Cook was among the first who established the poisonous nature of these seeds, because he was aware that those who had eaten them fresh fell ill as a result. He fed the pigs in the camp with these seeds and observed that some animals died. He later learned that the Aborigines used the seeds as a staple food with impunity. He found their secret method of preparation of the seeds, which involved the seeds being ground, steeped in water, and dried again and only then eaten without ill effect. The seeds of various cycads are poisonous and Aboriginals who use them eliminate most of the poison first. However, the seeds are still toxic and are even suspected of causing cancer in humans.

The thick stems of certain cycads are also useful as they contain enormous amounts of starch. To extract starch the whole trunk is cut down. Cycads occur on various Pacific Islands, and during the Second World War, when food was scarce, the Japanese restricted the use of this plant in the conquered territories to keep a steady food supply for their own soldiers.

A few Japanese soldiers lived for seventeen years in the remote jungle of Guam Island, hiding themselves after the war was over, as they did not want to surrender. They admitted that they had survived on the native cycads.

Cycads often have very attractive, large, stiff leaves, which are ideal for making wreaths or other decorations, as they are long lasting. The inhabitants of the Ryukyu Islands sell the leaves of cycads in large quantity to the West, and make a living from the simple activity of gathering leaves.

The ancient plants are known for their very slow growth and their appearance does not seem to change for years. There is a cycad (*Dioon* species) which was found to be 1000 years old, but is only 2 m tall. Small wonder that such ancient and beautiful plants are in great demand

Cycad
Encephalartos sp.

Black boy
Xanthorrhoea sp.

as ornamental trees, particularly the rare species. These plants are so coveted by collectors, especially in South Africa, that a specimen of an old cycad, *Encephalartos woodii*, was stolen from Durban Botanic Garden and was said to have sold for $65,000. To prevent the complete extinction of rare cycads, South African authorities prohibited the export of these plants. But unfortunately the illegal trade still flourishes. International action should be taken to save these magnificent and rare plant treasures.

The world's oldest cycad was believed to be the *Macrozamia denisonii* which grew near Brisbane, and was estimated to be 3000 years old. This magnificent cycad called Father Peter and measuring 18 m high was destroyed about twenty years ago. It was native to northern Queensland where many other cycads of this species can still be seen.

Pharaoh's Wood

Among the most handsome trees that nature has created is certainly the cedar of Lebanon (*Cedrus libani*). With its characteristic thick and large horizontal branches spreading a considerable distance, it has a unique pyramidal shape. Small wonder that the tree became the symbol of Lebanon and appears on the Lebanese flag. The cedars grow in the mountainous region of Taurus and Antitaurus in Lebanon, and in the past large forests of cedars covered the region. The oldest cedar still growing is some 40 m tall and about 4 m in diameter, and is estimated to be 4000 years old.

Its wood was considered to be imperishable in ancient times as it does not rot and is resistant to insect attack. Because of its quality and appearance the cedar wood was in great demand, especially for building palaces and temples. In the Old Testament this wood is known as being 'excellent above all trees in the field'. It was regarded as a symbol of prosperity, power and long life. King Solomon's temple was built of precious cedar wood in about 1000 BC, and the story says that at that time some 80,000 wood cutters had to be employed by the king to provide sufficient timber for this remarkable temple.

Cedar timber was not only in great demand as a building material but the fragrant wood was burnt as incense in the temples. The aromatic oil isolated from this wood was used by ancient Egyptians to rub over the body after bathing. It was also an ingredient of the most expensive perfumes and cosmetics for the nobles.

In ancient Egypt some thousands of years ago, cedar wood was used for making royal coffins and was also employed at that time for building barques and ships to be used on the Nile.

Cedar timber has great power to preserve itself. In 1954, during the excavation of the base of the Great Pyramid in Giza in Egypt the archaeologists who unearthed old cedar timbers, were greatly surprised still to be able to smell the aroma of 'the vapours of the wood, sacred wood of the ancient religion'—the timbers imported to Egypt over 4000 years before. The cedar wood timbers which were used for building the Pharaoh's funeral boat some 4600 years ago remain almost intact. A sacred boat made of cedar wood was buried near the Pharaoh's tomb by his son for the use by the dead in the life thereafter. This indicated that the myth about the imperishable nature of cedar of Lebanon wood was not a fable.

Unfortunately, large cedar forests have been destroyed in the past. These magnificent trees can now only be seen near the village of Becharre where some 400 trees grow in a special forest reserve in the mountains of Lebanon.

Black Boy

Among many fascinating plants which only grow on the Australian continent, are grass trees (*Xanthorrhoea* species). Although they are not real grasses, they have narrow leaves, forming a large clump and, from a distance, they resemble grasses, especially when the plant is young. But old specimens have a thick stem resembling a trunk up to 3 m tall on the top of which appears a large clump of leaves. The plant is most attractive when in bloom—from the tuft of leaves a remarkable narrow spike grows up to 3 m long, covered with thousands of tiny white flowers. In areas where many such flowering plants can be seen, it makes a great impression and no similar plant is to be found anywhere else in the world. In some regions grass trees are the most characteristic feature of the Australian countryside.

These plants seem to enjoy a calamity such as a bush fire and, when other plants perish, the grass tree not only survives but, starts producing flowers as if it had been waiting for such an event. In an area decimated by the fire, these plants raise magnificent spikes which, from a distance, look like white candles. Once the bloom is over, the spikes darken because the seeds are black. From a distance a grass tree in bloom or in fruit resembles an Aboriginal boy holding up a spear. The tuft of leaves on the top of the the trunk is likened to a boy's head of hair. As a result, the plant, which is common in Western Australia, is popularly called a 'Black Boy'.

One expedition became interested in the use as a medicine of a resin which oozes from the trunks of old black boys. As a surgeon named Smith recorded in his diary, 'Collection of a large quantity of yellow balsam from the tree which grows in large numbers on the sandy hills near Botany Bay . . . at least this balsam possessing medicinal virtue . . . in the same cases where they would have used the Balsam of Tolu or many other medicines in pulmonary disorders.'

Although grass tree resin was occasionally used in tincture form to treat dysentery in the past it has never become a medicine in Australia. The resin was of great importance to the Aboriginals, however, especially for attaching stone axe heads to wooden handles. For this purpose the brittle resin was heated in a fire.

When white settlers came to Australia, they started collecting the resin as well, since it was useful as a varnish.

The resin of some species is a strong red colour, and was used as a paint to disguise cheap timbers as the more expensive red cedar. The resin was sometimes used for the production of picric acid which could be converted into explosives. It is said that before World War I, up to 1500 tons of grass tree yellow resin was exported to Germany.

Various methods of extraction of the resin for commercial purposes were used. The most common was heating the plant pieces to melt the resin and collect it. Up to 2000 tons of resin was processed in 1934 on Kangaroo Island alone.

In the past there were even projects for exploiting the cheap resin for production of gas which was expected to be useful for lighting, but the project has not been further developed. As the dried resin burns off giving an aromatic odour, it is used as an ingredient of incense used in churches in Australia.

The grass trees grow very slowly and a 30 cm tall plant may already be 100 years old. Specimens with thick trunks may be several hundred years old. Some authors believe that some black boys may be 1000 years old. It should be noted that the grass tree is not a real tree and the 'trunk' is actually formed by the bases of detached leaves.

9.

Incredible Flowers

Monstrous Flower

One of the most remarkable plants ever found is the rafflesia (*Rafflesia arnoldii*) native to the tropical jungle of Borneo and Sumatra. As it is a parasite, this plant has no leaves, stem or root, and consists of one single flower of an incredible size. As it can reach 1 m in diameter, it is in fact the largest flower in the whole plant kingdom. And it is also the heaviest as the flower can weight up to 7 kg!

This monstrous flower was discovered in the interior of Sumatra in 1818 by Arnold, the British explorer. And this is how he described the event:

> I rejoice to tell you, I happened to meet with what I regard as the greatest prodigy of the vegetable world. I had ventured some way from the party, when one of the Malay servants came running with wonder in his eyes, and said, 'Come with me, sir, come. A flower, very large, very beautiful, wonderful.' I immediately went with him about a hundred yards in the jungle, and he pointed to a flower growing close to the ground, under the bushes, which was truly astonishing . . . To tell you the truth, had I been alone, and had there been no witnesses, I should, I think, have been fearful of mentioning the dimensions of this flower, so much does it exceed every flower I have ever seen or heard of . . . It measures a full yard across!

The monstrous flower does not really resemble any other flower. It has five large petals up to 1 cm thick, arising from the enormous nectarium which can easily hold a few gallons of liquid. The flower is brilliant red in colour, and its surface is covered with dirty-white patches so that the flower resembles rotten meat. In addition, it emits an intense and unpleasant carrion-like odour. Small wonder that such a flower lures swarms of carrion-loving insects. The insects assist in the pollination of the flower. So there is a good reason for this masquerade.

The monstrous flower remains open for only four days, when it changes and loses its 'beauty'. The whole flower gradually disintegrates and after a time it becomes a slimy and most unattractive mass. But before the flower vanishes completely the seeds develop. Thousands of tiny seeds are embedded in the slimy mass, and they can be easily distributed by various animals. Even the elephant is believed to be involved in the seed dispersal as elephant's faeces are often observed near the mature flower.

The development of the giant plant is fascinating too. It can only

Rafflesia arnoldii

Corpse flower
*Amorphophallus
titanum*

Star of Madagascar
*Angraecum
sesquipedale*

Aristolochia ringens

grow on the root of a particular species, the genus *Cissus*. Once the sticky seed lands on the root of the host plant, it penetrates the root bark and develops unseen inside the host tissue. After a time the parasitic plant bursts through the bark and appears as a small bud on the root surface. This bud gradually grows and takes some nine months to reach full size. The bud resembles a large cabbage head rather than the bud of a hidden flower. The giant bud eventually opens to reveal the flower's 'beauty'.

The rafflesia is a great botanical curiosity and not many people have had a chance to see it in bloom. It is in fact the dream of many botanists to see this unique plant in bloom. Special expeditions are organised with the sole purpose of rediscovering this plant. In 1964, Dr Zahl, a well-known explorer and scientist from the *National Geographic* magazine, penetrated the tropical jungle of Borneo, but was unable to find the plant at the right stage of development. Finally, he was lucky to find a giant plant in bloom. He was astonished by what he saw. He wrote:

> On the mammoth vine grew a flower that was virtually the size of a washtub. Its deep-set tissue glowed yellowish-orange like coals of a banked fire . . . here on the southern slopes of Mount Kinabalu, on the dark floor of an enchanted jungle was one Rafflesia not born to blush unseen.

As the full development of the giant flower takes exactly nine months, the natives of Malaya, not surprisingly, saw a striking resemblance between its development and human pregnancy. The rafflesia plant, especially its buds, were used as a sexual stimulant and a fertility charm. It is customary in some areas for women to give a rafflesia plant potion to their husbands to improve their sexual power. As the giant rafflesia is rare and very difficult to find, other related rafflesias are often collected for this purpose.

To prevent the extinction of this real botanic treasure of the Malaysian forests, a special national reserve has been established in the forests where this plant grows. There is a chance now that this remarkable plant will be preserved for future generations.

Corpse Flower

In the tropical jungle of Sumatra grows one of the most spectacular plants in the world. It is *Amorphophallus titanum* which bears one of the world's largest inflorescences. Dr Adoardo Beccari, who discovered this giant plant in 1878, was most astonished when he saw a flower some 2.5 m tall. He wrote:

> To give an idea of the size of the gigantic flower, it is enough to say that a man standing upright can barely reach the top of the flower,

and that with open arms he can scarcely reach the top of the spadix with his hands . . . and that with open arms he can scarcely reach half way around the circumference of the funnel-shaped spathe from the bottom of which the spadix arises.

The plant he found was in fact not a single flower, but a huge inflorescence, as the plant is a typical aroid member. The scientific name given to this unusual plant was fully deserved, as the huge spadix arising from the top of the spathe can be likened to a human penis of enormous size. The Latin name *Amorphophallus titanum*, means 'huge human penis'. The central spike of the plant in bloom hides thousands of flowers, both male and female, but these can only be seen when an opening is cut in the spike.

This most attractive 'flower' holds another surprise. It exudes a repulsive smell like rotten meat, and for this reason this plant is also known as the 'corpse flower'. Some naturalists describe this smell as a mixture of rotten fish and burnt sugar.

The tuber from which the giant inflorescence arises is enormous. It may weight up to 35 kg! Its only leaf is also enormous and can reach over 4 m in length. Small wonder that its discoverer had considerable difficulty bringing the specimen he found from the jungle to his hut. The giant plant had to be lashed to a long pole, the ends of which had to be placed on the shoulders of two strong men.

Although the plant is most spectacular when seen in the shade of the tropical jungle, it can occasionally be seen in bloom in botanic gardens. The flower is a great attraction to visitors—crowds gather to see the monstrous flower, the largest flower in the world as the media usually describe this inflorescence.

The giant aroid was successfully raised from an imported tuber, and it first bloomed in Kew Gardens in 1881. The pleasure of observing the giant flower was evidently spoiled by the smell which, it was said, was so repulsive that some people fainted inside the conservatory. They were advised to look at the giant through the window. Similarly, in 1937, when the plant began to flower in the Botanic Gardens in New York, it created more public attention than the opening of the opera season. Some people were patient enought to observe the event for four days until the final collapse of the monstrous flower. Flowering of this unusual plant was such a sensation in Hamburg one day, that 'a police cordon had to be made to control those who wanted to see the famous flower.'

Of course the plant's repulsive smell is not to repel people; its purpose is to lure insects to assist in the pollination of the flowers hidden in the huge inflorescence. In the forest the most common pollinators are carrion-loving beetles.

Some authors also claim that elephants may assist in the plant's pollination. Elephants are often observed visiting the huge flower to drink water which accumulates in the enormous spathe. Here the elephant unwittingly rubs pollen on to its forehead, and so the pollen is transferred to the stigmas of the female flowers. If this is true, it is an example of a remarkable cooperation between two giants, one from the plant and the other from the animal kingdom.

Giant of Peru

In the Peruvian Andes grows one of the most remarkable bromeliads, *Puya raimondii*. Although it is a herbaceous plant it has a trunk up to 4 m in height. The plant looks most unusual when in bloom. It produces an inflorescence which may be up to 5 m tall and some 100 cm thick and is the largest inflorescence in the plant kingdom. This inflorescence comprises some eight thousand individual flowers and is strong enough to support a man if he climbs it with a long ladder. Enormous energy is necessary to produce such a huge flower, and the plant only does it once during its entire life, and then dies.

Puia raimondii

The magnificent spectacle can be observed very rarely as the plant needs 150 years to reach the stage of development at which it blooms.

Not many botanists have had a chance to see this unusual giant plant in flower. Foster, a well-known explorer of the Andes, tried to find a blooming puya for several years, making special expeditions from the

Passion flower
*Passiflora
quadrangularis*

Hand-flower
*Chiranthodendron
pentadactylon*

USA, until finally his efforts were fruitful. This is what he wrote: 'No man living remembered when this plant was born for the event took place a century and a half ago, no one could have seen it bloom, for it does so but once in a lifetime'. We know now that the plant can bloom between its eightieth and one hundred and fiftieth year.

After his discovery, Foster returned home, but a few months later he decided to go back to collect the seeds. To his surprise the giant plant had disappeared. Natives set fire to the giant plants after they bloom.

Shepherds hate the plants because, when young, the low spiny leaves blind sheep when they run through the valleys. Thus, young puyas are often cut down to prevent such accidents.

Star of Madagascar

In the tropical forest of Madagascar grows a most unusual orchid, known as the star of Madagascar (*Angraecum sesquipedale*). It bears a very large flower, waxy and perfectly white in colour, and has a surprisingly elaborate 30 cm long spur. As it was the longest flower spur ever seen when it was discovered, the orchid was named 'sesquipedale' which means one and a half feet, relating to the dimensions of this unique flower.

Naturalists who studied the plant were amazed and could not explain how the nectar, which only fills the bottom of this enormous spur, could be reached by any insect. It was hard to imagine an insect having a sufficiently long proboscis to reach the nectar. Darwin also became interested in the newly discovered orchid in 1862. He postulated that since such an unusual plant exists, there must also be a moth which has a sufficiently long tongue to probe deep enough into the spur of the flower to collect the nectar and thereby pollinate the flower. As no such insect was known to entomologists at the time, the great scientist was widely ridiculed.

Nearly forty years later, however, a moth was discovered in the forest of Madagascar which had a tongue measuring exactly 30 cm, to match the orchid's spur. To commemorate Darwin's prediction, the newly discovered moth was named *Xanthopan morgani praedicta*—'the predicted'.

The reason this insect remained unknown for so many years is that its life span is very short, and it can only be seen at night. Fortunately the orchid remains in bloom for several weeks and therefore there is always a chance for the insect to meet its orchid.

A similar case but in reverse occurred in South America. This time, a moth with an unusually long tongue was discovered, but there was no orchid to match the moth. Again, several years later, an orchid (*Habenaria* sp.) with a long spur to exactly suit the moth was discovered.

It might be thought that such an unusually long proboscis would severely restrict the moth's flying capacity. Fortunately, when not in use, the long proboscis, is rolled into a tiny coil, so nature solved that potential problem well.

It is still a matter of dispute whether it was the flower that developed the enormous spur to match the insect's long tongue first, or vice versa. The most probable explanation is that during the long process of evolution both the plant and the insect have met to assist each other.

Pelican Flower

Among plants that trap insects but do not cause any harm to them are various birthworts (*Aristolochia* species), native to tropical regions of America. Their flowers are often very large and attractive. The largest are those of *Aristolochia grandiflora*, which attain some 50 cm in diameter, and are equipped with a pendulous tailed fringe, some 60 cm long. When the flower is not fully expanded it can be easily likened to a pelican, hence the common name of the plant—pelican flower.

The flower's structure is just like an eel-trap as inside the corolla tube there are inward facing stiff hairs which prevent the escape of a visiting insect. The entrance to the flower is an attractive red colour, often with brown spots bordered with yellow to make the landing platform more attractive for the insects. In addition, the flower emits a smell like rotten fish, which is most attractive to insects. Once the insect penetrates the heart of the flower, the plant, as one author pointed out 'seems almost to delight in listening to the bee beating its wings against the wall of its prison as it tries to escape'. After some time, the insect will have pollinated the stamens with a golden dust of pollen grains, and the plant is satisfied with visitor's performance. The flower's stiff hairs now wither and allow the insect to escape unharmed.

Some *Aristolochia* plants have a special adaptation by which the flower directs the way the insect penetrates its labyrinth. In the wall of the flower tube there is a special transparent area which the trapped insects see as a means of escape. But it is in fact a light to lead the insect towards the stigma to assure pollination. It is a remarkable adaptation, in which the plant controls the insect's movement inside the flower.

The odour which the plant produces to attract carrion-loving insects is so strong that it lures other animals. Wild pigs and domestic pigs, which are known for their strong sense of smell, easily detect the odour of this plant from a considerable distance. The animals relish the whole plant and even dig out the roots and consume them. But such a feast could be lethal. It has been reported that domestic swine 'who were attracted by the smell of the giant flower, perished from eating the roots'.

We know now that the roots of *Aristolochia* plants, which were formerly used in folk medicine, are highly toxic, and have even caused cancer in experimental animals.

Passion Flower

When the first Spanish Jesuits stepped ashore in the New World they noticed there a plant (*Passiflora* species) with most amazing flowers. These zealous clergymen took the flowers to be symbols of the crucifixion of Christ.

The flower's five sepals and five petals could symbolise ten faithful apostles—Judas who betrayed and Thomas who doubted were evidently omitted. The five stamens symbolised the five wounds of Christ. The three stigmas of the style were seen as the three nails, one used to nail each hand and one to nail the feet to the cross. The ovary of the pistil symbolised the hammer with which Christ was nailed to the cross. The showy corolla of the flower symbolised the crown of thorns, and the tendrils were said to represent the whips with which the Saviour was scourged. The palmate leaf was a symbol of the brutal hands of the Saviour's tormentors.

White flowers symbolised the purity of Christ, and the red ones his blood. As the flowers often only bloomed for three days, this was seen as a symbol of Christ's resurrection.

Little wonder that Spanish Jesuits saw this plant as the most convincing illustration of the Lord's suffering on the Cross. The plant was seen as a good omen; they hoped that the pagans in the new land would eventually be converted to Christianity.

The plant was called *Flos Passionis* (passion flower) and was soon taken back to Europe where its remarkable symbolism attracted many religious people. Simone Parlasca was most impressed by this plant and in a special book, offered to Pope Paul V, he was the first to describe the unusual symbolism of the passion flower.

The fruits of the passion flower also had some religious connotations in Mexico. When the missionaries saw natives drinking the juice extracted from the fruit, they considered it to be a strong sign that these people were 'thirsting' for Christianity, as they had chosen to drink from this most 'sacred plant'.

Some parts of the plant, such as the stems and leaves can be used to induce a remarkable calming action. The extract of certain passion flower plants has been used as a remedy to treat nervous tension and sleep disturbances. Since, however, the plant contains substances that can cause hallucinations, it is now less commonly employed in herbal medication.

African tulip tree
*Spathodea
campanulata*

Adam's needle
Yucca filamentosa

Sinister Hand-flower

When a Spanish expedition arrived in Mexico in 1787, they were surprised to see a tree in full bloom (*Chiranthodendron pentadactylon*). Its canopy was so unusual that the expedition leader was reluctant to report its discovery to Spain as he expected to be ridiculed for it. Little wonder, if we imagine, from the top of the tree, thousands of blood red human hands stretching in all directions. With distinct fingers and nails they were very sinister as they resembled hands covered with blood. We describe here, of course, the unusual flowers of this tree, and the fingers are in fact five large stamens and the nails are their pollen sacs. There is no other tree with such unusual flowers; no wonder it is called the hand-flower tree.

In ancient Mexico this remarkable tree was held sacred. It was believed that it was created by the gods to bring the people good luck. Strangely, it was thought that propagation of the tree would offend the gods, and for this reason the community removed all the flowers on the single tree in the area where it bloomed. This halted the formation of seeds and hence prevented further propagation. But the collected flowers were not destroyed. They were dried and commonly used as amulets to bring good fortune. They were also believed to have remarkable healing power. Most dreadful diseases, such as epilepsy, the cause of which was a mystery in those days, were treated with a potion made from hand-flowers.

It was later found that hand-flower trees were quite common in some remote regions, but the cult of the single tree remained unshaken.

The peculiar trees are also native to Guatemala where they are called monkey's hand, but enjoy no special veneration. The hand-flower tree is still regarded as a great botanical curiosity, and the tree is often grown in botanic gardens.

Flame of the Forest

Among the plants found in tropical forests of West Africa, the most spectacular is the spathodea (*Spathodea campanulata*), a medium sized tree which is most attractive when in bloom. Its large, brilliant scarlet flowers resemble the finest quality tulips, hence the plant's name the African tulip tree. When the flowers are in bud they look like small reddish banana fruits massed together. They do not all expand at the same time. Only the outer buds open, while the flowers inside remain closed. When the open flowers are spent they fall to the ground and then the inner row begins to bloom. In this way the canopy of this tree always seems to be covered with attractive tulips and the spectacle continues for several months. When the blooming tree is observed from a distance it looks as if it is on fire and is often called the flame of the forest.

The attractive fleshy flowers lure sunbirds which assist in pollinating the flower as they search for nectar. But the visitors are often frightened by the unexpected behaviour of the flowers. When touched by a bird, the flower squirts it with a nasty smelling liquid secreted by the inner part of the flower. This peculiar behaviour has been noticed by the natives who call it the fountain tree. The fruits which follow the flowers are attractive food to tropical bats, which come in crowds at night. Such feasts are accompanied by an unpleasant, and for some, most unbearable, cracking noise. As the concert is repeated with the same intensity every night, small wonder that those who want undisturbed sleep dislike the beautiful tree. And this is why this formerly popular tree began to lose its appeal. In some parts of Africa, the inhabitants are officially warned by the authorities not to plant this tree too close to hospitals, schools or private residences.

Another disadvantage is that the tree is not strong enough to withstand heavy storms, and often falls down.

In some parts of Africa the flame of the forest tree is associated with witchcraft. For example, in Gabon there is a custom of placing its flowers in front of the hut of a man who has broken a tribal taboo. The flowers are also put in the grave of those who have been executed for serious crimes because it is believed that the plant has the power to prevent the deceased's spirit returning to his body.

Adam's Needle   An American native plant called Adam's needle (*Yucca filamentosa*) is a well known ornamental plant with a rosette of stiff leaves terminated with needle-like spines. When in bloom, a showy tall inflorescence covered with attractive white bell-shaped flowers rises from the rosette of leaves. These flowers have fleshy petals which are edible.

The attractive flowers would not produce seeds without the assistance of a tiny, white moth which is the only vector for the plant's pollination. This moth (*Tageticula yuccasella*) lives in symbiosis with the plant.

The female moth is attracted by the smell of the yucca flowers at night. When she lands on the flower, she collects the pollen from the stamens and forms a large ball which she holds above her head. With this ball the insect then flies to another flower where it performs its complicated task. With its long ovipositor the moth lays its eggs in the ovary of the flower and then, as if knowing what would be the best thing to do, she deposits pollen on the top of the pistil, thereby pollinating the flower. By doing so, the tiny moth ensures that the pollinated flower will develop ovules in the ovary which in turn will serve as food for its larvae. In this peculiar way both food and shelter for her offspring are assured. The hatched larvae have plenty of ovules to eat, and as only a few eggs are deposited, some ovules remain intact to develop into seeds. In this way both the insect's and the plant's needs have been remarkably satisfied.

The symbiosis is so unusual that early naturalists doubted the truth of this story. How, they asked, could the moth know that if she laid any more eggs inside one flower, all the ovules would be destroyed by hatching larvae and the plant would die out. But the tiny moths seem to know how to make the symbiosis work perfectly. As each generation of insects behaves exactly the same way, and they learn nothing from their mother whom they never see, their behaviour must be an instinctive response.

It is interesting that other related moths which have probably observed the strange behaviour of the real yucca moth, also try to take advantage of the yucca plant. These moths also lay their eggs inside the yucca plant flowers, but they unfortunately 'forget' to pollinate the flowers. By such negligence their larvae starve to death as no ovules develop without pollination. As a result, their imitation does not work at all.

Underground Orchids

Orchids are famous for their incomparably beautiful flowers. It was, therefore, a great surprise to naturalists when certain orchids in Australia were found to live underground. It seemed incredible that the orchid flowers could live a normal life buried under the soil, never seeing the sun.

The first of two underground orchids was discovered in 1928 in Western Australia and was found accidentally by a farmer while ploughing his paddocks. The plant was identified as a peculiar species of orchid and was named the western underground orchid (*Rhizanthella gardneri*). It is a small leafless plant consisting of a stem some 3 cm long and numerous tiny flowers forming a head about 2 cm across. As the orchid contains no green parts it cannot assimilate its own food and so grows in association with certain underground fungi.

This underground orchid develops its flowers and bears seeds, always completely buried beneath the soil. The flower head may rise slightly as it grows so that it almost reaches the surface of the soil. Sometimes small cracks appear above the flower head. The tiny flowers emit a sweet odour which attracts underground insects such as termites. The plant does not try to distribute its seeds when they ripen and the seeds remain closed in the fleshy ovary. Some authors assume that the orchid's seeds are eaten by certain animals and are then distributed with their faeces.

The second orchid species which chooses life underground is the eastern underground orchid (*Rhizanthella slateri*), found in 1931. It was discovered in Queensland several thousand miles from where the first underground orchid was found.

10.
Peculiar Seeds and Fruits

Nature's Nasty Joke

One of the most famous plants in the world is *Lodoicea maldivica*, a handsome palm, native to one of the Seychelles islands in the Indian Ocean. This palm bears the world's largest seed. One seed may be up to 40 cm across and may weigh up to 18 kg.

It is not only the seed's enormous weight which fascinates naturalists but also its unusual shape and general appearance. It resembles a woman's pelvis both from the front and back and is the most peculiar structure ever seen. Small wonder that the early, more puritanic botanists who saw this seed called it the 'nasty joke of nature'.

Linnaeus, who named the plant, however, saw it in a somewhat different way. Evidently impressed by the remarkable sexual appearance of the nut, he called the plant Lodoicea, after the most beautiful daughter of the legendary King Priam of Troy.

The origin of the giant nuts used to be clouded in mystery. They were occasionally fished out of the sea by sailors near the shores of India, but their real origin remained unknown for hundreds of years. As they resembled double coconuts, they were called coco-de-mer, meaning sea coconuts. It was believed that the nuts grew on mysterious trees in underwater gardens in the sea near Java. It was claimed that these peculiar trees occasionally appeared on the water surface, but whenever a sailor wanted to collect the nuts, the trees disappeared under water. The trees were said to be guarded by monstrous birds with lion's heads and eagle's wings, and that many brave sailors had become victims of these creatures.

Small wonder that the mystery captured people's imagination. Soon the famous nuts became known as an effective aphrodisiac, as well as a cure for all ailments. It was also believed that the unusual nuts could counteract the most powerful poison. It was thought that when drink or food was placed in an empty nut shell any poison which may have been secretly added, would be destroyed. Indian maharajas and European kings, who often feared being secretly poisoned by their rivals or enemies, were usually ready to pay any price in order to possess the miraculous nut. King Rudolf II of Austria, for instance, proposed to pay 4000 gold florins for a single nut, a fortune at the time, but his offer was turned down. Similarly, another European king actually offered a ship full of precious goods for just one miraculous nut.

The possession of the famous nut used to be the privilege of monarchs and aristocracy. In the East Indies, for example, an ordinary

Coco-de-mer
Lodoicea maldivica

Breadfruit
Artocarpus communis

Match-box bean
Entada scandens

Monkey dinner bell
Hura crepitans

man found in possession of the precious nut was severely punished by cutting off his hand.

When, however, the palm tree bearing the famous nuts was finally discovered in 1768 on Praslin Island of the Seychelles, the myth was destroyed and the price of the nuts dropped immediately. Despite this, the giant seed with its mysterious history and sexual connotation, still remains a great botanic curiosity. It is a proud possession of some natural history museums where the famous palm bearing the world's largest seeds is a great tourist attraction.

The giant seed needs seven full years to mature. When the fruit is mature it drops to the ground and it is unwise to rest under the trees. Export of the famous nuts is strictly prohibited, and the palms in fruit are under constant guard on the island to prevent smuggling of the precious seeds.

Not only the seeds but also the flowers have a distinct sexual connotation, since the flowers, which occur in long catkins, can be likened to male sexual organs. According to a legend, love-making takes place in secret during a windy night between male and female flowers. But according to this legend 'one should not try to observe this event as he who witnesses the scene, dies forthwith'.

Among the first admirers of this unusual palm was British General Gordon when he visited the Seychelles. He was so astonished with these magnificent plants that he proposed to name the valley where they grew the Garden of Eden.

Breadfruit

First travellers coming back to Europe from the South Seas brought incredible stories about Tahiti where bread grew on trees. They must have been impressed with the unusual tree (*Artocarpus communis*) as it bore large fruits, the flesh of which was baked in an oven and tasted like the bread eaten in Europe.

The British authorities became interested in such a useful plant, known as the breadfruit tree as it could easily be used as a staple food, especially for slaves working on sugar plantations. An expedition was soon organized and in 1787, *HMS Bounty* sailed from England to Tahiti under the command of Captain William Bligh. The object of this long journey was to collect 1000 breadfruit tree seedlings and transfer them to Jamaica to be planted there.

After the ship reached Tahiti it took the crew five months to collect and load the young trees. But the sailors were so enchanted with the astonishing beauty of the native girls and the happy life on the island that their secret desire was to remain there for ever. Although they obeyed the ruthless captain, there was insufficient water for the crew as most of the water supply had to be used for watering the seedlings. The sailors decided to mutiny, and the rebels threw away all the precious plants. Captain Bligh was abandoned, with a group of his followers in a boat about 6 m long, with some food and water and with a sextant for navigation. The mutineers sailed to Pitcairn Island where they began a new life.

But the stubborn captain survived. After an incredible voyage of some 6000 km in a small boat he reached Timor, and was then able to return to England. Here he was court-martialled for losing his ship, but was found blameless.

Captain Bligh was ordered to make another expedition to the same island, and this time he was entirely successful. Although the breadfruit tree was planted to become a staple food for slaves working on sugar plantations in Jamaica, it never became the expected bonanza as the natives did not like the new food. They preferred plantains and bananas instead.

Some of the mutinous sailors were captured later and sent to England where some were tried and executed. Today, descendants of the mutineers still live on Pitcairn Island. And, Captain Bligh later became Governor of New South Wales.

There is a related plant (*Artocarpus heterophyllus*), native to India, which although not connected with such exciting stories as the breadfruit, also produces remarkably large fruits. This tree bears fruit which can weigh up to 25 kg. The tree looks most unusual when in fruit and, so is often planted as a curiosity. The fruit is not like bread however, and its golden-yellowish flesh can be eaten raw. In Brazil it is cultivated on a large scale; known as jack fruit, it is called 'poor man's bread', as this fruit is the staple food of the poor in some regions.

Jack fruit may occasionally reach an enormous size, and gigantic specimens measuring up to 90 cm long have been recorded. These giant fruits hang on thick peduncles directly from the main trunk of the tree and not from the branches. Some authors regard this as the largest fruit to grow on trees.

World's Largest Pod

Among the most interesting plants found in tropical forests is a woody climber, *Entada scandens*. This plant bears giant pods which may reach one and a half metres in length, a real record in the plant kingdom.

When the giant pods hang from the top canopy of the trees where the mother plant climbs, the impression they give is spectacular. Each pod is flat, woody, hard and grey in colour, and is only some 10 cm wide. The pod contains up to fifteen seeds which are embedded in separate compartments. When the fruit is mature it breaks into distinct segments to release its seeds.

The attractive seeds are disc-like and a glossy reddish brown, about

Bottle gourd
Lagenaria siceraria

Cocoa tree
Theobroma cacao

Durian fruits
Durio zibethinus

Viper's gourd
Trichosanthes anguina

6 cm in diameter. In the past, wax matches were commonly used in Australia. These matches were ignited by striking a rough surface and these handsome seeds were made into matchboxes. Hence in Australia the plant was called the matchbox bean. In tropical regions the attractive seeds are made into bracelets and ornaments and are often offered for sale to tourists.

The roasted seeds were formerly used by Aboriginal women in Australia as a contraceptive. The way they were applied was somewhat peculiar, as the women had to lie down and remain motionless for the whole day after taking such a remedy. The seeds are toxic when eaten in large quantities, but in Africa the roasted seeds are occasionally used as a substitute for coffee, although they do not contain caffeine. The seeds make a froth when shaken with water and throughout Malaysia they are used as a kind of shampoo. The stem has the same property and it is used in the Philippines as a soap substitute. The stem is cut into strips, pounded flat and dried. The strips are then soaked in water and rubbed to make a lather.

Seeds from the giant pod are occasionally found on European sea shores, thousands of miles away from the African coast where the plant grew. This indicates that the floating seeds must have been carried by sea currents from Africa.

It is not only the enormous size of the pod that is unusual, as the whole plant bearing them is unique. It is among the world's longest known stems of some 140 m. As the plant must exert enormous pressure to pump water in such a giant stem, when the stem is cut water sprinkles from it and can be used in an emergency.

Certificate of Virginity

Some plants produce fruits which cannot be eaten, but still serve a good purpose. Such are the fruits of *Lagenaria siceraria*, a climbing plant native to tropical regions. Its fruit is bottle shaped and commonly used as dishes in tropical areas. Hence the plant is called bottle gourd. By simply removing the pulp and seeds from the fruit, opening the 'neck' and drying it, one has a ready-made bottle. It is hard, robust, and light, and so can still compete with heavy, breakable glass bottles. The inhabitants of tropical regions have never had a problem with bottles or kitchen dishes as they have always had these fruits at their disposal. The fruit differs greatly in shape and size and some are more like huge sausages than bottles. Some fruit reach an enormous size and can be more than a metre long.

In East Africa bottle gourds are commonly used by Masai tribes, as they are easy to carry. They use the bottle gourds for storing milk, which they usually mix with cow's blood. This favourite and most nourishing drink is the main food of the Masai men when they cover long distances with their herds. To keep the liquid cool the bottle is covered with a leather coat, which is often richly decorated.

In the past, when the natives of Polynesia travelled by boat to neighbouring islands where sweet water was scarce, they took large bottle gourds with them filled with water.

Bottle gourds are used for making rattles and various musical instruments and they are often sold as souvenirs to tourists. In parts of South Africa small bottle gourds have a rather unusual application. The members of the Venda tribe, unlike other tribes, require that girls should preserve their virginity before marriage. In a special school, called the Domba sex school, girls who are soon to marry are prepared for their new role by experienced old women teachers. When the training is complete the girl's virginity is also tested by the teacher, and then a most peculiar school certificate is given to each girl—a small bottle gourd. If the girl's bottle gourd's neck is intact, it means that the girl is innocent; if, on the other hand, it is cut off, the unpleasant message is clear. As such a certificate must be offered by the girl to her groom just before the wedding night, the message provided could have a devastating effect.

The bottle gourd plant is assumed to be native to Africa. As it has been known in America since time immemorial, it must have been transported somehow to that continent. Special experiments were performed to show the possibility that a bottle gourd full of viable seeds could have drifted on the sea current from one continent to another. The fruit's hard shell makes it an excellent seed container, so such a belief is highly plausible. It is assumed that once such a gourd reached the American coast, somehow it broke open and released its still viable seeds giving rise to a new plant.

Another plant should be mentioned here, the so-called calabash tree (*Crescentia cujete*), native to tropical Africa. It bears very large and almost ideally oval fruit up to 50 cm in diameter. When the fruit is cut in two and emptied, it forms an ideal dish in which to keep water or food. It can also be used as a wash basin. The tree bearing these unique, large fruit is very attractive and is often planted as a curiosity in botanic gardens. Calabash shells are also used as souvenirs and musical instruments and are often used by native artists who decorate them. In tropical Africa large calabash dishes are commonly used as containers for local palm wine which is often sold on the roads between villages.

Xerxes' Fig

The fig tree (*Ficus carica*), which bears pear-like, edible fruits, has an interesting history. Native to the Mediterranean region, this plant was held in great esteem in ancient times. The fruits were in such demand that the Romans tried to conquer land in North Africa where the best figs grew. The emperor Cato was most unhappy that he still did not control the African coast where the precious fig trees were cultivated. Once, the story says, he brought a few figs into the senate meeting and declared: 'I would demand of you how long it is since these figs were gathered from the tree?' When the senators replied that the fruits were so fresh, that they must have been recently collected, Cato said: 'Yes, it is not more than three days since the figs were gathered at Carthage, so near is Carthage to our shores'. With this declaration to the senators, the emperor easily persuaded them to begin the Third Punic War. Plants have rarely been the cause of war, but the Romans believed the fig was an offer from the god Bacchus to mankind in order to make their life more joyful.

Fig
Ficus carica

Also Xerxes, the king of Persia, was known to be particularly fond of figs. When he was defeated by the Greeks at Salamis in 480 BC he was not so much frustrated about losing the battle, but because he could not conquer a land where figs were grown. He made a peculiar order to his servants. At every meal figs were to be offered to him to remind him that he still did not possess the land from which they came.

As the fruits are pear-shaped, they can have some sexual connotations. In the past, fig trees were regarded as a symbol of fertility. A giant phallus which was carried during the Dionysian festivals in Athens was carved from fig tree wood. Ripe fruit covered with candy to resemble human phalluses, were traditionally sold in Japan at autumn festivals at the Shinto shrine in Kyoto. The fig tree was also attributed with the power of bringing peace and of calming animals. It was customary to tie a fig branch around the neck of a bull, no matter how wild, to tame the animal. A fig leaf was used in paintings to cover people's nakedness.

Papaw
Carica papaya

Sausage tree
Kigelia africana

Figs are most peculiar in that they are not real fruits, but fleshy receptacles for numerous tiny flowers. These flowers are pollinated by a minute wasp, 1 mm long, the only insect that can get through the narrow opening of the ripening fruit. The tiny insect lays its eggs inside the fig, which provides food and shelter for the offspring and the symbiosis between plant and insect is most complicated. What is interesting is that no fruit will develop without a wasp. Cultivated figs no longer require insects to be pollinated as their fruit ripen without pollination, but it was a great problem for fig cultivators in the past. When, in 1890, fig tree plantations were established in Turkey, the insect which was brought as a pollinator did not suit the plant. The plants remained fruitless for some ten years until a suitable insect was finally discovered.

Food for Gods

The cocoa plant (*Theobroma cacao*) is a gift to mankind from Central America. The ancient Aztecs were the first to make a chocolate drink by pounding cocoa seeds and boiling them with water. They cultivated this plant for millennia, and it was the Aztec word chocolatl which was later changed to chocolate to make the word easier to pronounce in Europe.

The Spanish were the first to learn about the famous beverage when they landed in Mexico. When in 1519, Cortes was entertained at the court of Montezuma, the Aztec emperor, he was given 'chocolatl' to drink. As one Spanish historian wrote: 'I saw them/servants/bring in over fifty large pitchers full of fresh froth made from fine cocoa and he/the king/drank of it, the women serving him with great reverence . . .' They learned later that the cocoa seeds were given to the emperor as a form of tax by the people living in a moist Chiapas jungle, where the cocoa plants grew wild. These seeds used to be of such great value in Central America that it was customary to use the seeds as a form of currency instead of money. For example, in Nicaragua, a rabbit was sold for just ten cocoa seeds, while one hundred seeds 'would buy a tolerably good slave'. Cocoa was expensive and only rich and noble men could afford to use cocoa regularly, as it was literally 'drinking money'.

The Spanish conquistadors did not like the cocoa drink, and initially they abstained from using it. It was the Spanish missionaries who first became attracted to the Aztecs' famous drink. When they learned about its stimulating and nutritious value, they became virtual addicts of this native Mexican drink. It became customary for the padres to take a calabash filled with the cocoa drink with them as they wandered from one remote Indian community to another, saving souls, and converting the Indians to Christianity. For those hard-working missionaries the cocoa drink was their only pleasure. In order to have a steady supply of the precious seeds, the missionaries cultivated cocoa trees near their premises, and they became so involved in this agricultural activity that not much time was left for their missionary work. Angry bishops ordered them to sell the farmlands to stop this time consuming activity. They said they had to eradicate 'a crop from which the foaming cups of delicious and mind-refreshing drink was obtained'.

The chocolate we eat today was the invention of C. J. van Houten of Holland who developed the process of making chocolate in the early nineteenth century. The first bar of milk chocolate was made in 1876 by M. D. Peter in Switzerland.

Although the cocoa tree is a gift of the American continent, almost half the world's production of the precious seeds comes from Africa. Ghana (formerly Gold Coast) is the main producing country. Cocoa was introduced to Ghana some one hundred years ago by a humble smith called Tetteh Quarshie. He smuggled viable cocoa seeds from Fernando Po, where cocoa plantations had been established by the Portuguese. As cocoa is now more valuable to Ghana than gold, the grateful citizens commemorated the smuggling of the first cocoa seeds by establishing a hospital in Mampong in honour of the smith.

The cocoa tree is unique in that its fruit is borne on the main trunk and not at the end of branches, as in most plants. It is a small tree with almost white bark and resembles a birch tree. It bears an enormous number of very tiny white flowers. Up to 100,000 flowers may be counted on one tree, but of this only a tenth of one per cent will develop and form fruit. When the fruit matures, they are like bright yellow cucumbers hanging around the trunks. As the trees grow in the shade of taller trees, they form a 'miniature forest in which hang thousands of golden lamps—anything more lively cannot be imagined'. Linnaeus must have been impressed with this remarkable tree as he named its genus '*Theobroma*' meaning the 'Food of Gods'.

Stinking Delicacy

Accounts of the famed durian (*Durio zibethinus*) reached Europe as early as 1640. Durian is an evergreen tree which bears large spiny fruits the size of a man's head. The fruit when ripe is filled with white creamy pulp, resembling white cheese, which is as delicious in taste as the finest cream. Travellers to Malaysia said often that to eat durian is a sensation worth a voyage to the East. However, the delicious fruit has a most unpleasant odour, described by some as a 'mixture of onion and decayed meat', and for some it was a 'French custard passed through a sewer pipe'.

One traveller described his experience with durian in the following way. 'When it is brought to you at first you clamor till it is removed.

If there are durians in the next room to you, you cannot sleep . . . To eat it, seems to be the sacrifice of self respect; but endure it for a while, with closed nostrils, taste it once or twice, and you will cry for durian thenceforth—even—I blush to write it—even before the glorious mongosteen'.

Most people who have tried durian say that 'perseverance brings great satisfaction. To eat durian is to learn to like it; even though the nearest thing to it in consistency and flavour would be a mixture of melting mousse and garlic'. But for some people the smell of the durian is so intolerable that they could never try it. It is a real problem if one of the family hates durian and another loves it, there have even been cases of divorce.

Those who have enjoyed the unique pleasure of durian often suffer later, because the fruit leaves such a persistent odour that even taking a bath does not always help. Small wonder that posters in some Malaysian hotels remind visitors that bringing durian to their rooms is 'strictly forbidden'. Durian 'lovers' are so easily recognised from afar by their odour that they are often not even allowed to board their plane or ship.

When the fruit ripens on the tree it attracts various animals, especially monkeys, who are fond of the fruit. If the tree grows in the forest elephants are said to be the first to come and eat the delicious fruit. In some parts of Malaysia where the durian is a common tree, in order to prevent the loss of the whole crop people guard their fruit by building a shelter on top of the tree. As a traveller wrote: 'they build shelters in the tree, above the reach of elephants, whence they can descend by the ladder to pick up the fruits as they drop. Tales there are of Malays, who gathered a fruit only to be gathered in turn by an elephant'.

As the ripe durian fruit cannot be stored, even under refrigeration, for a long period of time, it can only be tasted where it grows. It is still worth travelling to South East Asia just to try durian. If it is true that, as Malaysians say, the fruit has a sex invigorating power, this could be another reason for some people to decide to travel to Malaysia.

Cannonball Tree

Early travellers exploring the tropical jungle of Brazil were occasionally surprised when instead of the roar of wild beasts, they heard a cannonade, or rifle fire, in the distance. They were surprised also when they learned that it was the noise of a certain tree. This tree (*Couroupita guianensis*), native to South American forests is unique in that its fruit make a lot of loud noise. The fruits are large and round, and hang on long peduncles. Whenever a strong wind blows, these iron-hard fruit, vigorously pound against the trunk or against each other. Little wonder that they can make a kind of cannonade which can be heard from a great distance—hence a common name for the tree, cannonball tree.

The tree is very attractive when in bloom. Its large waxy-white flowers up to 10 cm in diameter arise from long stalks and form large inflorescences. There are so many flowers on the tree that the whole trunk is literally covered with blooms and it looks like a beautiful column in a palace decorated with flowers. This tree is therefore most attractive, both in flower and in fruit and it is often cultivated in tropical regions as a decorative tree. There is one beautiful avenue of cannonball trees in fruit in the famous Botanic Gardens in Singapore.

There are other plants which may also frighten people by the noise they make, such as a tree native to South America. Known as the sandbox tree (*Hura crepitans*), it is often grown in tropical regions of Asia and Africa as an ornamental. Again the source of noise is the fruit, but this time the fruit explodes loudly when ripe. The explosion is so powerful that the seeds can be spread up to 14 m from the main trunk. The tree is popularly called the 'monkey dinner bell' a reference to the noise the tree makes.

The unripe fruit are round and flat, and, in the past were used for keeping sand to blot ink. For this reason the tree is sometimes called the sandbox tree.

Viper's Gourd

Another plant which bears unusual fruit is a member of the pumpkin family, a climber called the snake gourd (*Trichosanthes anguina*). This plant, native to China, has occasionally been cultivated in tropical regions for its edible fruit. People who have never seen a plantation before may be frightened when they approach as it looks as if the area is seething with hundreds of snakes. As the fruit are cylindrical and some 120 cm long and hang in coils from supporting sticks, they really resemble snakes. Depending on their stage of maturity, the fruits may be white, green or bright yellow and red in colour. Native people call the plant the viper's gourd.

In modern plantations the fruit do not look as attractive as in remote villages. To facilitate transport, the fruit are made to grow straight rather than in coils. To do this a stone is attached to the end of each fruit to weigh them down.

Establishing a new plantation is an easy job. The seeds are sown at the beginning of the rainy season, and bamboo sticks are placed to enable the new plants to climb. They grow very fast and the first edible fruits can be ready for harvesting after only three months. If one takes into account the fruit's great length, such a growth rate is quite remarkable.

The viper's gourd also has unusual flowers. They are showy and large and only open at night. Their corolla is composed of very peculiar almost hair-like fringed petals of a snow-white colour.

This plant hides another surprising quality. This time it is the root which was found to have an unusual power to suppress the development of the AIDS virus. The antiviral action of this plant is another fascinating secret of the snake-like fruit-bearing plant.

Jumping Bean

In the last century, so called jumping beans were famous in Mexico. They were offered to tourists and commonly sold in markets as a kind of amazing toy. When these beans were placed on the ground or on a table, they did not remain motionless but jumped about as if propelled by a supernatural power. As the plant bearing these unusual beans was unknown, the mystery surrounding the jumping beans survived.

The jumps the bean performed were not large, only a few millimetres high, but by doing so the bean could still cover some distance. When the tree (*Sebastiana palmeri*) was finally found to be the source of the miraculous beans however, this fame faded. It was discovered that it was not a bean but a seed, and that it jumped because of a small maggot inside. In other words, the seed was able to move because of an insect larvae which lived inside the seed.

It is quite an interesting association. A small butterfly, which has a special way of caring for her offspring, chooses the flower of this particular tree in which to lay its eggs before the seeds start to develop. Larvae hatch from the eggs deposited in the flower as the seed begins to develop. The larvae live comfortably and undisturbed due to an abundance of food inside the seed. But when the seeds ripen and fall, the maggots living inside lead a somewhat restless life. They vigorously change position inside the seed and this results in the peculiar jumping or hopping. In this way the seed slowly moves about and after some time covers a considerable distance from the mother tree. Some authors assume that the larvae instinctively know that remaining near the tree would mean attracting birds who would destroy the seeds. The larvae therefore keep propelling, their machines taking energy from the seed's inner wall which they constantly consume. What is interesting is that the insect larvae care for their homes. If a hole is made in the seed inhabited by a larva, it is closed immediately with a fine silky web. Jumping is disturbed for a while, but soon resumes. When all the food inside the seed is gone, the maggot chisels a fine opening in the seed coat and escapes to continue its development.

The jumping seed cannot produce a seedling as it is mostly destroyed by its former guest. Fortunately many seeds remain uninhabited and if they survive the attack of birds or rodents, they have a chance to germinate. Although it seems that it is only the butterfly who profits from the association, it is assumed that the insect assists with pollination when laying its eggs in the flower.

The Golden Tree of Life

Papaw (*Carica papaya*), also known as papaya, is a large herbaceous plant with a thick stem resembling the trunk of a tree, topped with an umbrella of very large leaves. Beneath the crown there are clusters of fruit which make the tree most unusual, as each fruit can weigh up to 5 kg, and there can be hundreds of such fruit hanging from the crown. Little wonder that the plant is often called the melon tree.

Not only is the papaya fruit delicious, but also, when they are immature they contain an enzyme, known as papain, which has a remarkable power of digesting protein. This enzyme also occurs in other parts of the plant, especially in the leaves.

In the Bahamas where this plant grows wild, people call the plant 'vanti' which means 'keeping well', because of its unusual ability to improve digestion after heavy meals. These people discovered long ago that they could eat as much of any fish as they liked without any ill effects provided they finish their meal with papaw fruit. They were also aware of another secret. When meat is wrapped in papaw leaves before cooking, the toughest meat becomes tender and delicious. This unusual property of the papaw plant has long been known to the Chinese, who have cultivated papaw from ancient times. As their poultry was often tough and hard to eat, they invented the most simple technique to tenderise them. They simply hung the newly killed bird among the leaves of a papaw tree, and this contact with the leaves made the meat tender. They also fed the birds papaw fruit before killing to make the meat more palatable and delicious.

It is exceptional that a plant containing a protein-digesting enzyme does not exploit this property for its own benefit like carnivorous plants. The power of papain is so great that one gram of pure isolated enzyme can digest two hundred times its weight of protein. Papain is now used medicinally as a digestive aid and was also used in the past to combat intestinal worm infestation. In this case the remedy simply digested the worms inside the body, and such a medication was formerly employed in folk medicine. Preparations of papaw should be used with caution internally as the enzyme may destroy the mucous membrane of the oesophagus if improperly used.

In the past when there was no refrigeration for meat and stomach problems were very common, powdered papaw leaves were an important medicine, so much so that the plant used to be known as the medicine tree.

Columbus, who learned about the remarkable property of papaw during his travels in America, recommended the use of fruit or powdered leaves for his sailors after meals to improve digestion. The famous explorer, Vasco da Gama was so impressed with the quality of this plant that he called it the 'golden tree of life'.

A peculiar property of the papaw is that a tree bearing only male flowers may suddenly produce fruit. They are usually very small and of a poor quality, but nevertheless they do occur. The reason for this unusual formation is that male flowers are sometimes hermaphrodite, having both stamens of male and pistils of female plants on the same tree. The papaw tree is dioecious; that is there are separate male and female plants and to bear fruit, plants of both sexes must be growing together.

Devil's Claw

Many plants produce fruits armed with hooks or spines to facilitate seed distribution, but none can be compared to the fruit produced by the grapple tree, *Harpagophytum procumbens*. This is in fact a climbing plant and not a tree, native to South Africa. It has a shell-like capsule, about 7 cm across, and is covered with 'fish hooks' like a special invention of nature to torture animals that meet it in the bush. Especially vulnerable are antelopes. One naturalist wrote: 'The luckless beast is fairly shod with this grappler, and many a weary mile must he limp along in torment before he has trodden the thing into pieces and pushed the seeds into the ground, and this is the way, at cost of much weariful agony to the antelopes, that the seeds could be dispersed'.

The fruit's hooks catch on all around the antelope's hock and every kick or scuffle drives the hooks further into the flesh.

Even worse is when an animal touches the fruit with its mouth. The fruits immediately attach themselves firmly to the animal's jaw. It causes horrendous pain to the animal, who cannot eat and is unable to rid itself of the object of torture. Even the powerful lion often loses its battle with this plant. Once the fruit becomes attached to his jaw, he is unable to hunt and some have been known to starve to death. Small wonder that the plant is called the devil's claw.

An interesting fruit which is equipped with a very long hook is the unicorn plant (*Proboscioidea louisianica*) native of America. When mature, the fruit end splits to form two curved hooks and looks most unusual. These fruits are supposed to be able to protect children against the so-called evil eye. In the Middle East, and especially in Irak, mothers use this fruit as an amulet against the evil eye by hanging the peculiar fruit round their baby's neck.

Devil's claw
*Harpagophytum
procumbens*

The fruit of the Unicorn
Plant
*Proboscioidea
louisianica*

Hanging Breasts
Another plant which bears most peculiar fruit is the sausage tree (*Kigelia africana*). Travelling through African villages people are often amazed when they see a tree from which huge 'sausages' hang in abundance. The fruits which are some 60 cm long and about 10 cm thick, hang on long ropes as if they were huge sausages in a butcher's shop window.

The natives of West and East Africa see the 'beauty' of this plant somewhat differently from the tourists who are simply surprised by its appearance. Ashanti people in Ghana call the tree 'nufatene' which means 'hanging breasts'. Such a name seems inappropriate and curious, but it is easy to understand when we learn more about Africa. Old African women, who are highly respected in the community, have often breastfed more than ten children and have unusually long breasts which they show with pride. The common African name for the plant is therefore quite understandable.

Although the fruit is not edible, because of its resemblance to breasts, the sausage tree fruit is regarded in many parts of Africa as a symbol of fertility. For this reason the sausage tree is commonly grown near houses in African villages.

This fruit cannot be eaten, but in East Africa the fruit pulp, which has an intoxicating effect when eaten, is used to fortify the locally made beer. In Kenya the seeds of the plant are believed to have the power to enhance men's sexual performance. The aphrodisiac property has not, however, been confirmed scientifically. Members of some tribes in Ivory Coast hang large sausage tree fruits in front of their huts as a fertility charm.

Underground Fruit
The peanut (*Arachis hypogaea*) is a native of tropical America. It has been cultivated in Peru from time immemorial. Peanuts were found in ancient graves of Peru, in 1877, and this indicates that the plant is not a native of Africa, as was once thought.

During the seventeenth and eighteenth centuries, when the infamous slave trade flourished and negroes were captured to be sold as slaves in America, peanuts were their main food during this long journey across the Atlantic. For this reason large plantations were established on the coastal regions of West Africa. So, the precious nuts, which are so commonly used now, used to have very sad associations.

Peanuts are also called earth nuts or ground-nuts and this is because of the fruit's remarkable habit of burrowing under the earth. This is most unusual behaviour for a plant and difficult to explain. What the plant does is most surprising. Initially it behaves normally and its flower stalk grows upwards as other plants do, but once the flower is pollinated the way it grows changes. The flower stalk bends and turns the immature fruit downwards to force it into the ground to a depth of 8 cm. The fruit then develop under the earth and it takes two to three months for them to reach full maturity. The fruit, known as pods, are then dug up like potatoes.

Fruit ripening underground was always regarded as most strange, and puzzled naturalists. Was it wise to place so many seeds together in one place instead of 'trying' to disperse them as other plants normally do? But the plant seems to have a reason. As it normally grows in semi-desert, planting many seeds in one place perhaps gives them a greater chance to survive. At least not all the seeds become the prey of animals and some seeds certainly germinate for the benefit of the species.

Peanuts have great nutritional value, and are popular, especially when roasted. Peanuts are also often used as animal feed. When peanuts were used as turkey feed in England in 1961, thousands of birds died mysteriously. It was discovered that the peanuts were the cause as they were contaminated with certain moulds (*Aspergillus* species) which produced very poisonous aflatoxins. It is well known that when peanuts are harvested during the wet season, fungi can attack the nuts. Since even roasting them cannot destroy the poison, it is wiser not to eat such peanuts. Aflatoxins are among the most dangerous liver poisons. They are also carcinogenic in laboratory animals, and potentially carcinogenic in humans.

11.
Unusual Water Plants

*Vegetable
Wonder*

Among the most spectacular plants ever found is the giant water lily (*Victoria amazonica*). This magnificent plant was discovered in 1801 by Thaddeus Haenke on the Amazon River, but his discovery remained unknown for 36 years as he was unable to publish his report as he died soon after completing his expedition. The plant was rediscovered in 1837 in the waters of British Guiana by another explorer and botanist, R. H. Schomburgh. Amazed with the unusual appearance of the plant, he reported:

> Some object on the southern extremity of this basin attracted my attention, and I was unable to form an idea what could it be; but animating the crew to increase the rate of their paddling, we soon came opposite the object which had raised my curiosity, and behold, a vegetable wonder! All calamities were forgotten; I was a botanist and I felt myself rewarded. There were gigantic leaves, five to six feet across, flat, with a broad rim light green above and vivid crimson below, floating upon the water.

No wonder he was surprised, as he had found the largest floating leaf in the plant kingdom. Some could reach a remarkable diameter of 2 m. The giant leaf has upturned edges to prevent water covering its surface, so it actually resembles a gigantic frying pan. The leaf is remarkably strong owing to a network of veins on its underside. One leaf is strong enough to bear the weight of a child without sinking, as if in a boat. It has been estimated that up to 70 kg, evenly distributed, can be held by the leaf quite well. In fact the structural principles of this giant leaf were exploited by the architects who designed one of the palm houses in Kew Gardens, London. Sir Joseph Paxton who was in charge, wrote: 'Nature has provided the leaf with horizontal and transverse girders and support that, I, borrowing from it, have adopted in this building'.

While the magnificent plant is a great attraction of various conservatories in botanic gardens, people in regions of South America are not so happy. The elegant water lily reproduces so fast that in some regions it has already become a noxious weed. One plant can produce 50 giant leaves in just one season. It is therefore not surprising that this plant can cover enormous areas. The plant is most difficult to control because spines covering both its leafblade and long leaf-stalk inflict injury when the plant is removed from the water.

Giant water lily
Victoria amazonica

Lotus
Nelumbo nucifera

The giant plant also bears magnificent large flowers up to 40 cm across, one of the largest known flowers. The beautiful flowers have some 60 petals and remain in bloom at night, emitting a pleasant scent. It is interesting that when the fruits form, they sink into deeper water in order to mature. Their greenish-black seeds are used as a food, and they are called water maize in South America.

Sacred Lotus

Probably no other plant is held in such esteem in the East as the lotus (*Nelumbo nucifera*). This aquatic plant, native to Asia, is among the most attractive water plants. It has beautiful, funnel-shaped leaves, which may be some 60 cm across, and stand well above the water surface. The plant also bears very attractive and fragrant flowers which can be up to 35 cm in diameter. The manner in which the plant rises pure and undefiled from the dirty mud, and the beauty of its flowers, suggest both purity and immortality. Little wonder that this plant was held sacred and became a symbol of beauty in the Orient.

The Japanese were most fascinated by the beauty of lotus plants. They amusingly describe the various stages of the flower's development. On the first day, they say, the lotus flower resembles a bottle of sake, on the second—a cup of sake, and a soup bowl on the third day, when its petals fall, leaving the flat body of the developing fruit clearly exposed.

Throughout the East, the lotus was viewed as the cradle of the universe. According to Hindu belief, Brahma the creator of the universe, turned the petals of the huge lotus flower into valleys, hills and rivers. An Indian fable holds that the lotus flowers obtained their red colour by being dyed with the blood of Shiva, when Kamadeva, the god of love, wounded him with the love-shaft arrow. The lotus is compared in India to their land—its numerous petals represent central India, while the leaves represent the remaining provinces.

Buddha is also associated with this unusual plant. He was believed to have been born in the heart of a lotus flower. Buddha is often represented in art as sitting either on a lotus flower or floating on its leaf. Also deities of various sects are represented on a lotus throne or are shown decorated with its flowers.

The lotus plant also has peculiar fruits. Unlike the fruits of other plants, lotus fruit are conical shaped and are flat at the top. The flat surface has numerous holes, each filled with a single nut-like seed. These attractive fruit are occasionally painted in gold or silver and sold as souvenirs in oriental shops.

The seeds of the sacred lotus became famous when their remarkable vitality was discovered. In 1951, Japanese palaeontologists found a few seeds in an excavated peat deposit in Manchuria. The seeds were found to be 1000 years old. Two of the seeds were still viable and when planted in moist soil they germinated. Amazingly, they produced healthy plants which bore beautiful flowers. A thousand-year-old seed produced plants which did not differ from those of the present day.

A related water plant, also known as the lotus (*Nymphaea lotus*), is native to Egypt. This plant is famous for its large and attractive flower, which was regarded as a symbol of purity and reincarnation in ancient Egypt. The flowers of this plant, known as the Egyptian lotus, were used during various religious ceremonies and the funerals of noblemen. Enormous masses of fresh lotus flowers, the story says, were used during the famous funeral of the Pharaoh Ramses II in 1237 BC. Wreaths of lotus blooms were laid in concentric semi-circles from the chin downwards so that the whole sarcophagus was filled with floral tributes.

It was customary in ancient Egypt to offer a lotus flower to guests when they arrived at noblemen's banquets. Each visitor had to twine the bloom into his hair or hold it in his hand as a sign of his peaceful intentions.

The lotus flower's aromatic scent was believed to have the power to protect any who breathed it—'flowers which have no equal'. Whatever the effect, seeing this plant in full bloom is certainly very pleasant.

Gift of the Nile

One of the most popular aquatic plants, in ancient times, was the papyrus (*Cyperus papyrus*). This giant sedge, with stems reaching 4 m in height, was the source of the earliest writing material in ancient Egypt some 5000 years ago. The Egyptians invented a method of making paper from the stems. It was usually prepared by slicing the inner parts of the stem into long strips. These were then lain next to each other and pressed to form large sheets known as papyri rolls. The papyri rolls were thoroughly impregnated with certain plant juices that made them immune to fungal or insect attack. Because of the ancient Egyptians' skill, valuable manuscripts have survived for millennia and considerable information about the history of ancient people has been preserved.

Among the most famous is the Papyrus Ebers, one of the oldest known works on medicine of ancient times (1550 BC).

Papyrus rolls were also used by the Romans. They were used for writing books and universally for correspondence and legal documents. According to Pliny, in the reign of Tiberius, the high price of papyrus rolls caused by the failure of the papyrus crop in Italy, threatened to disrupt business in the whole country.

The ancient Egyptians were masters at using papyrus for a variety of purposes. They used papyri for making mummy cases and also as the background for portraits to be placed over the mummy's face. Mummies of pharaohs were usually wrapped in papyrus sheets. Papyrus stems were also the principal material in the construction of light boats. Sculptures from the fourth dynasty show men building a boat with papyri stems cut from a nearby papyrus plantation. 'Vessels of papyrus upon the waters' were often referred to in ancient Egypt.

There is evidence that the ancient Egyptians, using their skill in building papyri boats, may have reached the American continent, although some scientists ridicule the idea. Thor Heyerdahl, a Norwegian explorer and adventurer, was convinced of the ancient Egyptians' skill, and he thought that such a possibility could not be denied. He decided to build a ship of papyri stems according to the ancient method, in order to try to prove the hypothesis. In 1969, he set sail with his crew across the ocean in a small papyri boat. In a most difficult journey he covered some 2800 miles towards the American continent, but a heavy storm forced him to abandon the trip. In May 1970 he made another attempt and this time he was successful. After 57 days his 'ancient' boat reached America, covering an incredible distance of 6000 km.

It should be noted that papyrus was also a food in ancient Egypt. The stems were either eaten raw or boiled to extract sweet juice. Papyrus was held in such great esteem in ancient Egypt that it became the symbol for protection against crocodiles. The plant became an emblem of Lower Egypt, where great plantations were established in ancient times.

Now the famous plant has become a weed in certain regions. For example, it dominates the waters of Lake Victoria in East Africa to such an extent that large islands of the plant disturb navigation. It is almost impossible to pass through papyrus forests in some areas of the lake.

Blue Devil

Among the most hated plants in the world is no doubt the water hyacinth (*Eichhornia crassipes*). This aquatic herb, native to South America, became a virulent water weed covering many water surfaces and making them useless. When this plant was introduced to the USA from Venezuela in 1884 it was regarded as an innocent and most attractive water ornamental, with its green expanded leaf-stalks and showy bluish flowers. But the plant soon escaped from private ponds and appeared in neighbouring rivers. As water hyacinth reproduces remarkably fast, it soon covered whole rivers and the plant mass was so dense and strong that people could walk from one side of the river to the other as if on a bridge.

A similar story occurred in Africa in 1951 when a missionary brought the beautiful exotic plant to the Congo and introduced it as an ornamental in his garden pool. Water hyacinths easily escaped, however. The plant first appeared in the Congo River and then found its way to the largest African river, the Nile. In some parts of Sudan water hyacinth formed into such great masses that it totally blocked naval communication. In

Papyrus
Cyperus papyrus

Water hyacinth
Eichhornia crassipes

some areas of the Nile, the river's flow has been so disturbed and slowed down that a ship which would normally take six days to travel from Khartoum to Juba, now takes twice as long to cover the distance. Lake Victoria has also been infested and in some areas communication by ship is very much disturbed.

The water hyacinth has also become a menace in India. Up to 3000 km of irrigation canals became useless because of blockage caused by the plant. Floating islands formed of masses of hyacinth are known to swamp and destroy entire rice fields. They often ruin fishing grounds and have even caused wooden bridges to collapse.

Water hyacinth is a very difficult weed to eradicate, especially before herbicides came into use. In the USA partial destruction of the weed was achieved by large scale use of arsenic poison. But countless numbers of domestic animals were also killed and many crops were poisoned and endangered. Even the use of powerful explosives such as dynamite did not kill the weed. Although the plant masses were blasted into small pieces and looked as if none could survive, just a few remaining pieces were sufficient to grow new plants. Ironically, these new plants were even stronger and healthier than before the blast.

Even fire was tried to eradicate the weed, but while the plants seemed to be totally burnt, a few still remained intact and grew again and faster. The most promising treatment was the use of biological control, and various organisms were tried, such as tilapia and even sea-cow.

On the positive side, it should be mentioned that the troublesome weed has an unusual ability to absorb various poisons from water, hence, it can be considered to be a water purifier. Because there is a great problem with worsening water pollution around the world, perhaps one day we will see the plant doing something good for the planet. It might be too early to condemn this plant as the evil weed.

Viviparous Plants

One strange water plant is found in the mangrove forests, growing in salty waters in subtropical lagoons. These plants are specially adapted to living in salty water which would certainly be deadly to other plants. Mangrove forests, which are best visited by boat, surprise all who see them for the first time. Only the tops of the trees can be seen at high tide when the sea is flooding the forest.

Different plant species make up the mangrove community. Some of the trees growing there have a most peculiar method of reproduction, unknown in any other plant in the world.

The most striking is the *Rhizophora stylosa* tree. When in fruit, sausage-like objects hang from the branches up to 60 cm long. These objects are in fact the developing seeds, which germinate while the fruit is still attached to the mother tree. From the pear-like fruit a hypocotyl of the seed slowly grows, elongating and thickening. Finally the sausage-like hypocotyls are too heavy for the branch to support them and, like a dagger, they plunge straight into the mud or water below. It is very unusual for seeds to germinate while still attached to the mother plant, and for this reason some mangrove trees are called viviparous plants. Strangely, the tree seems to know how to plant itself in such a way that it will survive and so produce a new plant.

By stabbing the mud with some force the heavy seedling penetrates the mud and by taking root can withstand the tide. If on the other hand the hypocotyl lands in the water, it floats on the surface and has a chance to take root elsewhere. If this plant produced normal seeds most of them would be carried away by the sea current and perish.

A seedling shoot of
Bruguiera gymnorrhiza

When the tide is out we see another peculiarity of the mangrove forest. Pencil-like projections stick up out of the mud around the trees. These are in fact the breathing roots which have to absorb oxygen from the air because of its deficiency in the salty mud.

Mangrove forest is also a unique sanctuary for interesting animals. Among them is a peculiar mudskipper, a fish which is able to climb branches of mangrove trees. They dance curiously over the mudflats to reach the tree and then climb up the trunk with the help of their strong pectoral fins. The fish has special water pockets which cover its gills to keep them wet so that they can breathe out of water.

There is an interesting mangrove forest in the Northern Territory of Australia. Visiting this area is not without risk, however, as deadly crocodiles which are known to kill people live in these waters. This risk can be avoided by using boats and not trying to approach the mangrove forest from the land.

12.
Bizarre Desert Plants

Octopus of the Desert

The strangest plant ever found was no doubt the welwitschia (*Welwitschia mirabilis*), and the specific name, 'mirabilis', meaning strange, is fully deserved. This unique plant was discovered by the explorer Dr Frederic Welwitsch during his trip through the Namibian desert in south-western Africa, in 1859. He was so overcome, the story says, by the unusual object he saw, that he 'knelt on the sand and did not move ahead and thought it was an optical illusion'. What he saw, was a round table, some 1.8 m across, rising up from the sand. On both sides of this 'table' two giant leaves, up to 6 m long, were split into a mass of ribbons. No wonder that when a drawing of the welwitschia was sent to Europe it caused disbelief among scientists.

Welwitschia mirabilis

Further studies of this unique plant revealed that although it is a tree with a distinct trunk, it cannot grow upwards and so only reaches about a metre in height. The growing power of the plant has been transmitted to its leaves, which never fall and continue growing throughout the plant's life. The two giant leaves, which are leathery and thick, become longer and thicker, and their ends fray at the ends, torn by the wind and scorched by the desert heat. The leaves grow from their base and increase in size very slowly, about 5 cm a year. Some welwitschias can be 2000 years old.

The trunk has dark brown and extremely hard wood, but without annual rings, and estimation of age is carried out by carbon-14 tests.

When the plant was taken to England, Dr Hooker, who was in charge of Kew Gardens said 'it was the most wonderful plant ever brought to this country, and the very ugliest'.

This remarkable plant is regarded as an anomalous relic of evolution. It only grows along the inner fringe of the coast of the Namibian desert, not more than 50 km from the shore, where the plant draws water stored in stream gravel after storms.

Dr Welwitsch, who died in London and was buried in Kensal Green cemetery, has the famous plant carved on his tomb to commemorate his discovery.

Ghost Men

In the arid zones of south-west Africa peculiar succulents from the genus *Pachypodium* grow. Because of their unusual trunks these plants are often described as misshapen trees. The most interesting is *Pachypodium namaquanum*, which is a small spiny tree some 2 m in height. As the trunk has no branches and is thick at the base, it resembles the figure of a man, especially when seen from a distance. The trees grow in groups in some areas, and at night they look like a group of men wandering through the desert. Natives are frightened by the unusual appearance of these trees, and they are reluctant to go to the bush at night, calling the trees night-mares or half-people. In some parts of Africa where these trees grow in large numbers they are called ghost men.

Peculiar stories are told in Africa about their origin. According to one 'the creator, taking pity on a band of Hottentots fleeing across the desert and wishing to protect them from their enemies, changed them into plants which could withstand the pitiless desert'. As the fleeing people were escaping in a northward direction they say, the crown of leaves on top of the trunk faces in the same direction. Although only a small crown of leaves appears on the top of the trees, when rain comes the ghostly trunks suddenly change their whole appearance. At the top of the tree tubular, reddish-brown flowers appear and the plant looks very attractive in its new garb. Small wonder that the Africans call it the desert rose.

The plant emits a strong scent of jasmine which can be detected a quarter of a mile away. The plant exudes a highly toxic milky sap when injured, and in some parts of Africa the sap has been used as an arrow poison. This plant has become rare and is now protected by law. Damage to plants is punished by a heavy fine.

Monstrous Cactus

The greatest cactus of all is the saguaro (*Carnegia gigantea*). Native to Sonora Desert in Mexico and south-western California, this giant can reach 16 m in height. An old giant cactus is an unusual shape. As its thick arms come out at the same height and then turn up it resembles a giant candelabrum. A giant saguaro is an enormous plant and may weigh up to 10 tons. To stand upright and to withstand violent storms the saguaro has a very strong skeleton which is a framework of hard cells running through the whole length of the trunk.

It has no leaves, but the outside shell of the stem is rich green and contains chlorophyll to make food from sunlight. Deep parallel ridges run along each arm of the cactus, with vicious thorns spaced along the crests. These ridges are firm and tough, but they can fold and unfold like an accordion. When it rains, the plant expands and takes in as much water as it can, unfolding and increasing in size. In a long dry spell, the pleats fold in and the plant simply shrinks.

So the giant cactus is well adapted to desert life as it can store enormous amounts of water in its stems. One giant cactus can become a water tower holding some 3000 litres of water.

The saguaro is well prepared for taking water. Its root system spreads out as a big water-collecting net up to 30 m, just below the surface of the soil. These roots keep on collecting water as long as there is a trace of moisture. This water supply has to last long periods of drought, often as much as two years.

Saguaro do not bear flowers until they are many decades old. They start blooming when they reach a height of about 6 m. Numerous waxy white flowers attract insects which assist in pollination and fruit soon follow. The crimson fruit are edible and they are usually picked by Indians using long poles. Climbing a giant cactus is risky because of the sharp thorns. These spines are some of the toughest plant material ever created, as they are practically unbreakable. But there is one animal which seems to enjoy climbing the giant cactus, despite its ruthless thorns. This relative of our domestic cat, known as the bobcat, has the miraculous ability to climb the giant saguaro without harm. He is able to place his feet against the sides of the spines instead of their needle-like points. This cat climbs the saguaro stem after bird's eggs, or just to rest before attacking small animals at night.

Saguaros grow very slowly. The plant is only some 0.7 cm tall after two years; at 15 years it is only some 30 cm tall, and after 40 years it reaches a height of 3 m. After 70 years the plant may be about 6 m tall and it is then that the plant starts branching. Mature plants are up to 200 years old.

Saguaro
Carnegia gigantea

Prickly pear
Opuntia sp.

Evil Cactus

The prickly pear (*Opuntia* species) is a well known cactus native to Central America. This plant, with characteristic flat leafless stems, and usually with long spines, is a source of juicy fruit. The plant was held in such great esteem in Mexico in the past that it was known as teonochtli—the goddess of the sun. A great temple was erected in its honour, and human sacrifice was a common part of religious ceremonies.

The prickly pear has an interesting connection with Australian history. It was introduced in 1788 by Captain Arthur Phillip, the Governor of NSW. He learned on his way to Australia that a certain parasitic insect of this plant could produce a valuable dye. It was the cochineal insect, from which a fabric dye was obtained on the Canary Islands. This was the reason why the governor brought the plant and some insects from South America, with the aim of establishing a profitable industry in NSW. But while the plant grew remarkably well in Australia, the cochineal insects did not, and the governor's idea failed.

But prickly pear soon escaped and spread. Because of the plant's heavy spines it could not be grazed by animals, so undisturbed it started to spread with astonishing speed. It soon formed such formidable hedges that animals were unable to enter their pastures. Those who tried to cut down the evil weed soon discovered that even the tiniest remaining part was enough for a new plant to grow, soon covering the land again and making it useless.

By 1925, over 60 million acres of land had been conquered by the plant and it advanced with an enormous speed over its whole range, devouring up to 100 hectares of land per hour. Over 600 different schemes were tried to stop the invasion of the new plant in Australia, but none was effective and the situation seemed hopeless. Finally a biological method of fighting the dangerous weed was tried. It was discovered that the larvae of a certain insect in Mexico (*Cactoblastis cactorum*) consumed a large quantity of prickly pear after hatching. To combat the evil cactus, some 3 billion insect eggs were brought to Australia and a big battle commenced. The results of the first trial were most promising when the eggs were spread on the cactus forests. The larvae had an unusual appetite. They consumed the prickly stems of the plant with astonishing speed, and where all other methods had failed, a tiny moth was able to win the battle. Millions of formerly useless areas were brought back to pasture or cultivation, and the evil cactus was defeated.

Queensland people were anxious to show their gratitude to the Mexican insect and erected the Cactoblastis Memorial Hall, in the small town of Boonarga. The emblem at the entrance to the hall can be clearly seen in large print over the entrance door.

It is interesting that although most animals are reluctant even to try and eat the fleshy stems of the prickly pear because of the spines, some animals can consume these plants with impunity. The Mexican javelina, a distant kin of the domestic swine, for instance, can easily blunt the spines and eat the plant, which is its favourite and provides both water and food.

Strange Boojum Tree

In semi-desert regions of lower California grows a most peculiar tree, known as the boojum tree (*Idria columnaris*). Early botanists called them the most amazing spectacle, describing them as court jesters, since the trees were so different from all 'normal' trees seen before. Its stem, which may be some 20 m tall, is an unusual shape, as from its 90 cm wide base, it gradually tapers to form a very thin, almost pencil-thin top. Most trees have no branches and from a distance resemble huge telegraph poles.

The tree may develop side branches but the way they grow and their shape is most unexpected and peculiar, unlike any other trees. The flexible narrow trunks may bend over and take root and the tree then resembles an artificial arch.

The trees are densely covered all over with short, thorny branches which are leafless during the long dry season. These queer trees occur in great numbers, forming forests some 300 km wide, and they survive under harsh semi-arid conditions. They are able to store enormous amounts of water collected during the rainy season, which they utilise when there is no water. The wood of the tree is fleshy—an excellent adaptation to the arid conditions.

Very old boojum trees are often hollow at the base. Bees often take advantage and make their nests inside the hole. In such a natural beehive up to one hundred pounds of honey may be found. Small wonder that Indians who discovered this secret, exploited the tree as a source of honey. They cut a plug at one side of the tree base and collected the honey. After it was collected, the plug was inserted again and left alone to fill again with the sweet contents. In fact, collecting honey from these trees became an easy livelihood for the Indians living near the boojum forests.

Another use for boojum trees has been found in some regions. Its thin stems are cut into 20-30 cm long pieces and are then hollowed and filled with melted wax to make excellent candles. Mexicans produce these candles on a commercial scale and export the wood and call the tree 'a long candle'.

But the Seri Indians who live along the coast of the Sonora Desert, regard the boojum tree as a bad omen. Whenever they find it growing in the vicinity of their huts, they destroy it.

Most travellers who have seen a boojum 'forest' are surprised when they return to the same area the following year and find that the trees have not changed at all. Even ten years is a short period as the boojum grows extremely slowly. It is often marvelled at, that all the plants seem to be of the same age and not a mixture of young and old. The explanation is that most seeds produced by the trees do not produce new plants as they are usually eaten by rodents which occur in great numbers. As a result, often, for several years not one new tree has a chance to develop. When the rodent plague finally disappears, many seeds germinate at the same time and place, and hence a forest of same-age trees can cover large areas.

Monstrous Tuber

Among various yams which occur in tropical regions, the most remarkable is *Dioscorea elephantipes*, which grows in the arid regions of South Africa. It produces an incredibly large tuber which may weigh up to 350 kg. This huge tuber is some 90 cm high and, as it is covered with angular corky protuberances, it looks like a huge tortoise walking through the sand dunes. During the dry season when the plant dies back, all that is left is this unusual tuber.

The huge yam is filled with a large quantity of starchy material, from which a kind of bread can be made, especially when other yams are not available. Hence, in South Africa the plant is known as Hottentot's bread.

The plant grows very slowly, only about one centimetre in three months, and it takes another eight years for the tuber to reach 8 cm in height. If the growth rate is as slow in the following years, one can imagine how old a plant must be to weigh over 300 kg.

Apart from this gigantic yam there are many species of yam which are edible. Yams are in fact a staple food in many tropical and subtropical regions and were already being cultivated in China by 2000 BC.

In tropical Africa and Malaysia, yams are cultivated in almost every village or community and in some parts of Africa they are virtually regarded as sacred plants. Special festivals are held annually when the yams are ready for harvest. These important celebrations, known in West Africa as New Yam Festivals, are actually thanksgiving ceremonies to thank the gods for the food provided. On the appointed day, the best yam tuber is collected and offered to the community chief, who after cooking it is the first to consume the new yam. Only after that ceremony is over can the new crop be eaten by everyone in the village. Eating a new yam before the festival is a deadly offence to the gods and the taboo is strictly obeyed. Cases have been reported of prisoners, starving themselves to death because news of the yam festival in their native village did not reach the prison in time.

In the past, as an act of purification, criminals were executed before the yam festival. In Nigeria, people were sometimes afraid to leave their home before the New Yam Festival, fearing that they might be captured

Boojum tree
Idria columnaris

and sacrificed to the gods.

In the Ashanti region in Ghana, yams were also used in departure ceremonies in which ancestors were worshipped by their relatives. During such ceremonies, which lasted three weeks, mashed yam was placed in front of the stool on which one of the deceased used to sit before death. This yam was known as soul food in Ghana. The yam crop is always regarded as strictly the property of those who care for the plants in the fields.

In Malaysia there is a peculiar custom evidently invented to discourage would-be thieves. The owner of the yam plantation secretly plants some highly poisonous yams amongst the edible yams. As the plants look very similar this method deters those who want yams without getting involved in their planting.

Some plants resemble huge tubers, but are not tubers at all. Such is a plant native to Kenya (*Pyrenacantha maldifolia*) which has a fat stem that resembles a huge tuber. Its succulent stem or trunk is some 1.5 m across and is filled with a fleshy and juicy pulp, and is particularly popular with elephants who often eat whole trees.

The Manna of the Bible

In the steppes and deserts of the Middle East and Asia inconspicuous crusty lichens of the genus *Lecanora* grow. These are in fact double plants, as the body of a lichen is a unique association of alga and fungus. In this symbiosis the fungus receives carbohydrates from the alga while the alga receives other basic food substances from the fungus. These plants are usually small and often circular in shape. When the crust develops it rolls up and then breaks into small pieces. These small pieces are easily carried away by rain water. Great masses of the crusty lichen may suddenly appear from nowhere. In some districts of Persia heaps of manna covered the ground up to 15 cm thick in 1828, and people thought it had been brought down from heaven. As the manna plant can be gathered in considerable quantities it is often a real blessing to people, during times of famine, as it can be ground and eaten. This lichen is supposed by some to be the supernatural bread which rained down from heaven and saved the Israelites from starvation after their flight from Egypt.

Lichens have astonishing adaptability to environmental conditions, as they survive extreme desiccation. They are known to go into a state of suspended animation and can remain in that condition for many months until the next rains. Lichens then absorb water at an amazing rate, and are known to increase their former weight over fifty per cent in just ten minutes.

Lichens are so remarkably resistant to extreme heat or cold that they can survive in the desert, tolerating over 80°C when dry. They also develop normally and continue to photosynthesise when frozen at -10°C in polar regions. These astonishing plants must have been the first to venture ashore in the beginning of the world. They were able to invade volcanic islands, growing on the old lava, as well as being perfectly adapted to living in the frozen tundra.

Lichens are an important source of food in the north, where lichen such as reindeer moss are the main diet of grazing reindeer. These tiny crusty plants, which can live almost anywhere, prefer to grow in unpolluted areas. Scientists even use this plant as an indicator of pollution. The tiny lichen have a remarkable power to absorb pollution from the environment. Long after the explosion of the atomic bomb in the Pacific during the Second World War, people living in northern regions of Scandinavia were found to have an unusually high concentration of radioactive substances in their bodies, although the polluted island of Japan was many thousands of miles away. No one suspected that it was the tiny lichen which were the source of pollution. It was revealed that the lichen, which accumulated large amounts of radioactive substances, was the main food of the reindeer, which in turn were the staple diet of the Scandinavian Laplanders. The reindeer moss was also harvested as a food reserve for the reindeer, which increased the chance of large amounts of polluted material being absorbed by Laplanders eating the reindeer meat.

These humble plants grow extremely slowly. One lichen discovered in Arctic regions which was not more than 10 cm in length was found to be 10,000 years old, according to the 1990 Guinness Book of Records.

Parakeelya

In the arid and hot regions of northern Australia, where not a single drop of rain may fall for two years, grows the broad-leaved parakeelya (*Calandrinia balonensis*). This plant often covers rocky soil, and is common around salt lakes. The parakeelya seems to enjoy the harshest environment, where no other plant can survive. Its fleshy and juicy leaves are thick and resemble grapes and are of particular importance to cattle as they provide both fodder and water. Cattle grazing on parakeelya can survive without water for years, although it seems almost incredible that a single plant can provide them with all they need. The cattle are perfectly healthy on their uncomplicated diet and produce normal offspring, just as in other areas where both pasture and water are available in abundance.

But there is a disadvantage in this relationship. Cattle bred on parakeelya fodder are not interested in drinking water and this is a real handicap as such cattle cannot be transported to a distant market. During the long trip, cattle must be watered at the water-holes on the way, but even when very thirsty, the cattle always search for their favourite plant rather than drink the water provided. The only solution is to teach the cattle the new skill of drinking water. To achieve this, the cattle are kept near a water hole and far away from the juicy parakeelya. It is a strange sight to observe the behaviour of an animal who has never seen water in its whole life. Water is completely strange to them. The cow smells the water at first, then paws it carefully, but lacking the technique of drinking, it cannot do much. The animal is often scared by the strange reflection of itself in the water, but soon becomes used to it. She then bites the water trying to eat it rather than drink it. When the cow finally decides to take a mouthful of water, she cannot swallow it at first and coughs it out. But she tries again and again and soon learns the technique of drinking and swallowing, first in small and then later in large mouthfuls. Soon the cattle are ready for the long trip.

Rose of Jericho

In the arid regions of the Middle East grows the rose of Jericho (*Anastatica hierochuntica*). This plant has a unique ability to change its shape. Normally, when there is enough moisture, after rain, its branches spread to form an attractive star and produce inconspicuous white flowers. After flowering and setting fruit, however, which occurs during drought, the whole plant starts to change its shape. All its branches curve in and form a kind of skeletonised hollow ball, which covers the fruits inside. The plant is easily uprooted and the ball is blown by the wind and covers large distances being rolled on the smooth desert sand.

Many such balls can be seen tumbling against the wind as if alive. As soon as the ball reaches a muddy place or when the rains come again, the plant changes its shape again. Its stems reabsorb the water they lack and assume their former spreading habit, as if starting to live again. Little wonder that the plant became known as the resurrection plant. The plant's strange behaviour also gave rise to its common name, rose of Jericho as it was believed that when Christ was born all plants expanded miraculously to greet the Saviour, this plant also became known as Mary's flower. It was customary to take this plant, in a ball-like form, home from the Holy Land after pilgrimages.

In some regions of the Middle East, especially in Palestine, the famous plant was regarded as having a special power to facilitate childbirth. When a woman was about to deliver, the magic resurrection plant was immediately searched out. It was put in a washbasin filled with water and placed in front of the woman. Once the plant miraculously expanded, it was believed the child would be born without problems.

Tumbling weeds are also found in arid areas of central Asia where some plants can form round masses as large as haystacks. Running with the wind through the steppes they often startle animals and people, especially at night. Many fables about ghosts seen at night should be attributed to tumble weeds. Small wonder that these plants are often called wind-witches. The famous rolling object which stunned Isaiah, as described in the Bible, is thought to be a *Gundelia tournefortii* tumbleweed, which often moves at high speed through the desert.

13.
Plants Worthy of Kings

Legendary
Myrrh

Myrrh is an aromatic resin obtained from the myrrh tree (*Commiphora molmol*) native to Arabia. It was among the most precious incenses of the ancient world and was among the gifts brought by the three wise men to Christ at Bethlehem.

According to an old Syrian legend, Myrrh was a daughter of King Thesis. The girl refused to worship Aphrodite and the angered goddess punished her by forcing her to commit incest with her father. She disguised herself for eleven days, the legend says, but on the twelfth night the king realised who she was. He was furious and chased his daughter, trying to kill her. To save the unhappy Myrrh from this revenge, Aphrodite quickly transformed her into a tree. Since then the myrrh tree exudes resin, to commemorate the king's weeping daughter.

As the resin was commonly burnt at the altars of temples, there was a great demand for myrrh in ancient times, especially in Egypt. The aromatic smoke was considered the only way to please gods. Large quantities of myrrh were used in mummifying the dead, especially noblemen and pharaohs. As there was a strong belief that the spirit of the deceased would return, all efforts were made to preserve the body to receive the spirit. Elaborate methods of embalming the bodies were invented. Herodotus described one method in the following way: 'The body was opened with a sharp stone knife, and after removing the contents of the abdomen, the cavity was washed thoroughly and then rinsed with aromatic infusions'. The body was then filled with aromatic myrrh and other precious spices. After the body was sewn up it was soaked in a solution of soda for 70 days. The body was then wrapped in linen bandages from head to foot, smeared with a gum solution and put in a wooden case carved as a likeness of the deceased. It was then placed in the sepulchral chamber.

At the temples of Heliopolis where the sun god Re was worshipped, myrrh was burnt three times daily. This resin was also among the precious gifts offered by the Queen of Sheba to King Solomon in 1000 BC. Myrrh is still used for making aromatic smoke during religious ceremonies, especially in the Roman Catholic Church. Myrrh contains an aromatic volatile oil with an antiseptic effect, hence the use of myrrh tincture as a gargle.

*Gift of the
Queen of Sheba*

In the Arabian peninsula and in Somaliland grows a small tree (*Boswellia carteri*). An aromatic resin that exudes from an incision in the bark is known as frankincense. This resin used to be so valuable as an incense that it was compared with gold and was among the famous gifts brought by the three kings to Jesus in Bethlehem.

Frankincense was in such demand in ancient times that the first recorded expedition ever organised specifically to collect a plant was for these precious trees. Queen Hatshepsut of Egypt ordered thirty frankincense trees to be found and planted around her temple at Deir el Bahari.

Frankincense resin was burnt at the most famous altars of Greek and Roman temples, and the rising smoke was regarded as the most efficient vehicle of prayer. Frankincense was believed to secure immortality, hence it was often burnt during the funerals of nobles and kings. An extravagant amount of frankincense, which was said to have been a year's production was burned at the funeral of Poppaea, the wife of Nero. Frankincense was also valuable during such ceremonies as its smoke masked the odour of cremation.

The demand for this resin was enormous and its price was so high that only nobles could afford the luxury. It was produced in Arabia and caravans loaded with the precious resin had to cover thousands of miles to reach Egypt where the cargo was transferred by sea route to Rome. The road which was used was treacherous as it ran through the most desolate semi-desert regions. The caravans often fell prey to marauders who attacked and robbed them; hence the road known as the Incense Road was in fact very dangerous.

Those kingdoms whose borders had to be crossed by the caravans of frankincense gained considerable wealth from taxes demanded from the frankincense merchants. Obstacles on the famous road, or disputes that arose, were often solved at the highest level.

When King Solomon created problems for the merchants using this road, the Queen of Sheba intervened personally. She covered thousands of miles with caravans loaded with precious gifts, and despite the harsh conditions, she was able to visit the king. When she arrived in his palace after this incredible journey, 'she communed with him of all that was in her heart' and King Solomon, the story says, was so moved by the event, that he allowed the incense route to be used as asked.

The price of frankincense was always kept high. Those who collected the resin from the trees in South Arabia, told incredible stories about the dangers involved. They said that wounding the tree to force it to exude the precious resin made the tree angry and it would emit a vapour which often killed the labourers. That is of course not true as the plant has no toxic properties at all.

Alexandria was the main sorting and processing centre of the resin collected and brought from Arabia. Strict security was applied: 'before they (the workers) are allowed to leave the premises they have to take off all their clothes' in order to prevent them stealing the precious frankincense.

Emperor's Fungus

No other mushroom assumed such prominence in ancient China as *Ganoderma lucidum*, known in Chinese as ling chih. This peculiar, antler-like, brilliant shining fungus has an interesting history. It was said to be discovered in 109 BC by the Chinese Emperor Wu Ti who found it on one of the interior walls of his palace. He was so astonished with its unusual appearance in the most unexpected place that he took it as a good omen and a gift from heaven. He must have been most impressed with his discovery as he ordered a special celebration to be held in honour of his remarkable fungus. Everybody, the story says, shared food and drink and he even granted total amnesty to all the prisoners in the country. Delighted with his fungus, the emperor was said to have composed a special ode in its honour which was always sung on official festivals in the palace.

It is not surprising that this fungus, so praised by the emperor, became a talisman of good fortune. It also became a symbol of longevity. According to a fable dating from the first century BC, a piece of this miraculous fungus carried by a raven had the power to give life back to a man who had been dead for three days. Such was the belief in the miraculous power of this mushroom that a special stone carving was erected during the Han dynasty. The carving was a replica of the fungus beneath two shamanistic figures.

The peculiar mushroom is usually a rich purplish brown or chestnut brown colour, and it always looks highly polished. It does not deteriorate when dried so it can be kept as an ornament almost indefinitely.

The reason the mysterious fungus appeared inside the palace was that the spores usually develop on the wood of old trees. The palace timber must have been made of very old wood, hence the Chinese emperor's surprising discovery.

The Root of Life

Ginseng (*Panax ginseng*) is the most famous plant of the orient. The root of this small herbaceous plant bears a remarkable resemblance to the shape of a man and so it is little wonder that the Chinese call the plant ginseng which means man-plant. Because of the unusual human-like form, the root was claimed to ward off any disease and restore exhausted powers, and even to have the miraculous power of making

Myrrh tree
Commiphora molmol

Ginseng
Panax ginseng

old people young. Ginseng is regarded as the remedy of harmony and an aphrodisiac and it has been used for over 5000 years in China.

Various legends are associated with the origin of this plant. According to one, the famous root was discovered in the Shensi province of China. The whole village was disturbed one night by a peculiar howling coming from the countryside. The people gathered together and went to see what was happening. They found a small herb which was screaming for attention. When they dug the plant up, they unearthed a strange, human-like root. They called it 'spirit of the earth' and since then its miraculous power and fame has never ceased.

According to another legend, a young and beautiful girl who was married to a nobleman could not become pregnant. She had a dream one night in which an old man ordered her to go to the mountain and to dig up the man-like root, from which she had to make a drink and take it. The girl did as instructed and after nine months she gave birth to a beautiful child. Hence the fame of the remarkable power of the root.

The ancient Chinese scripts are full of authentic stories confirming the unique healing power of ginseng. A case was described of a man who was close to death but when given a ginseng potion 'was sufficiently restored to carry on items of business'. Ginseng used to be so expensive that its value was a hundred times that of silver. Only monarchs had the privilege of using this precious medicine. It was a cure conferred by imperial favour only upon the highest officials, whenever 'they have a serious breakdown that does not yield to ordinary treatment'. It was said the ginseng root 'fills the heart with hilarity while its occasional use will add decades to human life'. It was believed that by using this root regularly, Chinese emperors would retain their youthful power.

The areas where the precious plant grew used to be guarded to prevent ordinary people obtaining the famous roots. Wars were even fought between the Chinese and Tartars over possession of land where ginseng grew. One Tartar emperor ordered a tall wooden palisade to be built around a whole province which was rich in ginseng plant, to prevent ginseng being stolen. In 1779, one Tartar emperor sent some 10,000 soldiers to the country to collect the roots and bring them to the palace.

It was believed that the ginseng plant shone in the dark and so should be looked for at night. It was customary to shoot a coloured arrow at the light, so that the following day the plant was easy to find. At one time in China those who collected ginseng root as a profession were often attacked by bandits known as white swains who robbed the collectors and often killed them.

Belief in the unusual power of ginseng was so strong in the orient that the Vietnamese were known to collect a piece of the miraculous root when going to the battlefield. When wounded, the root was used as an emergency drug as it was thought it helped to overcome stress and was often a real lifesaver.

It was formerly assumed that it was only because of its unusual shape that ginseng had the power of healing. We know now that the root contains various medicinally active substances. It looks as if God only created the root in this most unusual human form in order to draw mankind's attention to the plant.

14.
Crooks Among Plants

Plant Prostitute   The flowers of the orchids (*Ophrys* species) so strikingly resemble insects such as bees, that they are commonly known as bee-orchids. Their petals are folded like the wings of an insect at rest, and are sometimes even covered with velvety hairs to imitate perfectly an insect's body. What is most incredible is that the flowers are even known to emit an odour identical to that of the female insect.

Early botanists noticed with surprise that after landing on the insect-mimicking flowers, certain insects moved vigorously and remained there for some time. The botanists tried to explain this peculiar behaviour by saying that the orchid tried to frighten the invading insect in order to prevent potential damage to its flowers. But, the puzzle remained unexplained for many years.

Ironically, it was not a scientist but an amateur naturalist who solved the problem. Mr M. Puyanne from France, who worked as a judge in Algeria used to watch interesting plants, including bee-orchids, in his spare time. He was the first to come to the conclusion that the bee-orchid does not try to frighten the insect but, on the contrary, it wants to lure it to make love with the flower. He explained that the insect who lands on the flower makes the vigorous movements because he takes the flower for a female insect and tries to copulate with it. Meanwhile, the insect becomes covered with pollen and, by repeating the same movement on another flower, assists in the cross-pollination of the orchids.

But when the observant judge published his discovery in 1916, it was ridiculed by most botanists in Europe. They described his explanation as a fantasy of a dirty old man obsessed with sex. M. Puyanne had to wait many years before his ideas were published in a reputable journal and accepted in scientific circles.

Some puritanical botanists even accused the orchid of fooling innocent insects, by offering nothing but an empty promise, and they even called this orchid a plant prostitute. Others tried to defend the plant by saying that it is better to accept one lover than to invite different clientele, referring to other, less faithful, orchids. It is certainly true that the sexual desire of the male insect is never satisfied by its pseudocopulation with the flower, but if the insect were to achieve climax, the whole plan of the clever orchid would be a failure. An insect satisfied with his relation with the plant would not be driven to look for another flower and as

Bee-orchid
Ophrys fuciflora

Living stones
Lithops sp.

a result most of the orchids of this species would never be pollinated.

It is still a mystery how the insect-like orchid knows when exactly to invite its guests, because the orchids flower exactly when the male insects lack their own female partners. At that stage, the female insects have simply not yet hatched, so the orchid becomes the male's only lover. By the time the relation is over, the female insects have hatched and matured. Thus, in this clever association, the needs of both the plant and the insect are served very well.

Living Stones

In the arid regions of South Africa we can find some interesting plants from the genus *Lithops*. These small fleshy plants have no stems and only consist of two succulent, round leaves which are not green, but greyish, beige or almost white. As these plants grow between pebbles and rocks, it is almost impossible at first sight to distinguish the plant from the stone. Hence the popular name of such plants—living stones. Some plants which are grey even have characteristic white spots on their surface to match the pebbles among which these plants grow.

These living stones are small, usually not more than 2 cm across, and they are almost completely buried in the sand so that only the leaf-tops are exposed.

The plant has another interesting adaptation; its green assimilating tissue is not on the surface, as in other plants, but is embedded deep inside the leaf structure. Sunlight, therefore, cannot reach the chlorophyll to enable photosynthesis. Instead, the plant has evolved a 'window' of transparent cells through which the sunlight can reach the assimilating tissue. A very unusual adaptation.

What is this elaborate camouflage for? It is assumed that the aim of the plant is to increase its chances of survival, as their fleshy leaves would be the first target of browsing animals in a region where not many other plants survive the dry season. This camouflage certainly helps defend the plant from animals. But when the rainy season starts, this camouflage seems to lose its value completely. From a small opening between the two adjacent leaves, a long stalk arises and soon a showy, daisy-like flower reveals its beauty. By then the plant can behave normally, as with the abundance of grass and other plants, the living stones are entirely safe.

It is almost axiomatic that the smaller the plant the larger the flower it bears. The sudden appearance of flowers on the barren rock-covered soil, is met with surprise by the locals, who call these plants 'flowering stones'.

The plants also bear peculiar fruit which explode when ripe. The fruit burst and eject their seeds far away so that new plants can start their life elsewhere. The seeds also have special air-filled pockets which enable them to float in water. This again assists in their distribution. The tiny plant seems to have solved all its problems in a most clever way.

False Promise

To assure their pollination, some plants entice insects in a most elaborate way. For example, an African stapeliad (*Stapelia variegata*) bears an attractive flower which spreads out like a starfish. Its petals are mottled with reddish-brown spots resembling rotten meat. This resemblance is strengthened by a disgusting odour of carrion. Small wonder that, with such an appearance and smell, the plant easily attracts crowds of blowflies from afar, which lay their eggs in the flower, in the belief that the hatching larvae will find enough food in this carrion-like flower. But of course the hatched larvae cannot find anything to eat, and starve to death. The larvae are often seen crawling desperately on the petals but they find no food. It is a rare example of a plant deceiving insects by making a false promise but giving nothing back. Some naturalists say, therefore, that this stapeliad is a crook among plants. It simply needs to lure insects to ensure the pollination of its flowers, so in fact it cannot be held responsible for the fact that the insects have an exaggerated impression of what the plant has to offer.

Another stapeliad (*Stapelia gigantea*), which is famous for its showy, star-shaped flowers, which may reach over 45 cm in diameter, behaves similarly. Its attractive flower is clothed with purple hairs which make the surface of the plant look like velvet. This stapeliad also emits an odour of rotten meat to attract flies.

But not all Stapeliads deceive insects. Some, such as *Stapelia flavopurpurea*, native to the Karoo Desert of South Africa, emits a sweet, honey-like odour to attract insects to assist in the pollination of its flowers.

Sensitive Plant

There is no other plant in the world with such unusual feelings as mimosa (*Mimosa pudica*), a plant indigenous to Brazil but also found wild in many tropical countries. A popular saying 'as sensitive as mimosa' is fully justified. Indeed its reaction to touch is most unusual and surprising. At the slightest touch its leaflets collapse one after another along the leaf stalks, which also eventually drop into a relaxed position. Touching the plant seems to set off a chain reaction as the plant collapses all its leaves in just one tenth of a second. The irritation is transmitted in the plant over a distance of half a metre at a rate of some 10 cm in one second. After about ten minutes or so the irritation is over and all the leaves assume their original position as if nothing happened. The plant is now ready to react again at a touch. Small wonder that this plant became a botanical curiosity and that it was named the sensitive or humble plant.

Early botanists were puzzled by its behaviour and even thought that this plant had a nervous system similar to that of animals. We now know that the peculiar motion is caused by changes in the turgor pressure of certain cells surrounding the base of the leaflet stalks. Irritation causes the cells to lose water, and this in turn causes the leafstalk to collapse. When the irritation ceases, these cells reabsorb water and become as stiff as balloons, and the leafstalks assume their normal, upright position.

The mimosa plant assumes the sleepy position at night, when all its leaves collapse. Temperature changes also cause the plant to react; for example, when a flame is held near the leaf the plant reacts as if it was touched, immediately folding all its leaflets.

But the sensitive plant behaves differently when treated with a vapour of chloroform. It completely loses its reactions to touch, as though the plant forgets what to do under the influence of the anaesthetic.

Is there any advantage to the plant in such sensitivity? The sleepy position it assumes during heavy rain or hailstorms is said to help mimosa survive, whereas other plants' leaves are often severely damaged. Some authors also say that by the sudden change of position of its leaflets the plant removes various larvae attacking its leaves. By assuming its wilting and unattractive pose the plant may also deceive browsing animals who prefer to eat healthier looking plants and ignore mimosa.

The sensitive mimosa is often grown indoors or in gardens as a curiosity.

Another related plant, known as pigra (*Mimosa pigra*), which also reacts to touch by folding its leaves, is far from being admired in Australia— in fact it is now regarded as a noxious weed. This plant called giant sensitive plant, since it is a shrub some 6 m tall, was brought as a curiosity to the Darwin Botanic Gardens about a hundred years ago. It spread from the gardens and became a common weed in most waterways and rivers of the Northern Territory. The plant has nasty thorns and forms impenetrable hedges, blocking access of wildlife and livestock to many waterways, and is a serious environmental threat. Only by national action will this sensitive weed be controlled before it is too late. The pigra weed is probably as serious a problem now for Australia as the prickly pear used to be.

Stapelia sp.

15.

Animal-eating Plants

Venus Fly Trap

It is hard to believe that a plant which draws insufficient nitrogen from the soil has evolved an ingenious method of supplying this element from animal flesh. When the plants were first discovered, they were regarded as macabre.

We know now that there are many plants which catch and consume insects. The most bizarre among them is a small plant called the Venus fly trap (*Dionaea muscipula*). It grows in North Carolina and was discovered in 1760 by Arthur Dobbs, Governor of North Carolina. He likened this plant to an 'iron spring fox trap' when he observed it catching insects. He said: 'On anything touching the leaves they (the leaf-lobes) instantly close like a spring trap and confine any insect that falls between them.' Being an amateur botanist, he did not try to explain the peculiar behaviour of the plant. When the strange plant was shown to Linnaeus he called the plant a miracle of nature, but he remained unconvinced as to the 'insect eating' habit of the plant. He called it *Dionaea*, after Venus, a symbol of female beauty.

But, an American explorer, William Bartram, had no doubt of the 'meat-eating' habit of this unique plant when he wrote in 1793: 'admirable are the properties of the extraordinary *Dionaea muscipula*. Astonishing production! See the incarnate lobes expanding—how gay and sporting they appear! Ready on the spring to intrap incautious deluded insects! What artifice! Its hold sure, its prey can never escape—carnivorous vegetable'. Darwin, who was fascinated with this plant, called it the most wonderful in the world.

Seen in action for the first time, this plant is astonishing. Its leafblade consists of two distinct lobes, and the open trap looks like a sea shell with prong-like teeth. Its closing mechanism resembles a trapping device for catching foxes and it suddenly closes when touched.

The trap lures insects with nectar. Once the insect lands on the trap surface, the two lobes close rapidly together like a medieval instrument of torture and the insect has no chance of escape. The iron lady now starts its feast. It is a slow process and the digestive glands start to secrete the enzymes only after the prey is imprisoned and crushed. It takes up to ten days to digest and absorb the insect. Once this is accomplished the leaf blades open again and wait for new prey. The plant is only interested in fat insects, and if an insect is too small, the chamber does not close, and the insect is permitted to escape.

The plant's rapid reaction to touch is astonishing. At the centre of each leaf lobe there are a few trigger hairs which are sensitive to an insect's touch. Only when the insect touches these hairs is the signal triggered to cause the trap to close immediately. If someone only touches the trigger once, the plant memorises this stimulus and does not react until another touch comes within 20 seconds. Only an insect entering the trap can touch the sensitive hair more than once. According to some authors, this plant knows how to count. When it has the first stimulus it counts one and waits until the next stimulus comes. The plant behaves as if it were a computer as it distinguishes between a zero (no signal) and one, which it keeps in its memory. This unique mechanism is designed so that the plant avoids closing unnecessarily when a drop of rain or a speck of soil touches the trigger. The reaction to a proper touch is very rapid, as it takes only about half a second to close the chamber. According to some authors, this closure mechanism is based on electrical impulses created in the plant, but until now it has not been explained in detail.

It remains a mystery how such a plant could develop such an unusual device during the long process of evolution. Many experiments have been performed with this plant which is often cultivated by enthusiasts. It was found to accept a piece of beef, which it ate without problems, but a piece of cheese was too much and the trap died.

It is interesting that the peculiar plant can only catch and digest three insects during its whole life. After that it loses its hunting power as the leafblades wither. Fortunately each plant has a number of insect-trapping leaves.

Pitcher of Death

Travellers returning from Malaysia brought incredible stories about plants that supposedly ate both animals and people. They believed this as they had seen the famous pitcher plants which are carnivorous and can eat insects or small animals. Some are large enough to fit a hand into. A piece of meat thrown into it would be dissolved within a few days.

The trapping device these plants developed is formed of highly modified leaves that form a pitcher, with a distinct and often brightly coloured rim. Insects are lured by the nectar secreted by the inner wall of the jar. The waxy surface is as slippery as ice and once the insect lands on the rim it slides and falls to its doom. The bottom of the pitcher is filled with a liquid and contains special glands secreting digestive juices. The plant acts as a stomach and is able to digest all the soft parts of the insect's body and absorb its nutritious substances. In this peculiar way the plant obtains nitrogen which is lacking in the soil where the plant grows.

The largest pitchers are *Nepenthes rajah*, found in Sumatra. The giant jars are up to 50 cm in height. Such jars accumulate water during the rainy season and may contain up to two litres of liquid. This liquid is rather uninviting looking because of all the small insects found drowned in it. Sometimes a large pitcher may catch not only insects, but even larger animals such as rats or frogs.

As each pitcher contains some liquid they have been utilised occasionally as a source of water. Monkeys have been seen to drink from the pitchers, hence a popular name of the plant, the monkey cup. The liquid has also been a lifesaver for people lost in the jungle. Two British explorers in Sri Lanka once lost their way and their last water supply had gone and they were sitting in the forest awaiting inevitable death from thirst. Suddenly, a monkey which accompanied them, jumped ahead as if it had spotted something strange. With their remaining strength, the travellers followed the monkey and they were surprised to see a number of pitchers growing on the ground. The dirty liquid, although full of ants and other insects, was good enough to provide them with the necessary water to survive.

It is amazing that although pitcher plants are deadly enemies of all insects, there are some insects that take advantage of the plants. One is a spider, native to Singapore, which lives inside the deadly jar. By spinning its web just above the mouth of the jar, the spider catches insects before they find their way into the deadly well. When frightened this spider is known to dive into the dangerous liquid, but soon crawls back on to its web and resumes a position of vigilance. This spider must be immune, partly at least, to the action of the digestive juice found in the pitcher's liquid.

The larvae of certain insects can also live inside the liquid. Here they share the prey with the plant, consuming drowned ants or other small insects. So some insects find both shelter and food in the pitcher— a very interesting adaptation indeed.

Dangerous Sundew

The most popular insect-catching plants are various species of the genus *Drosera*. These often very small plants, commonly known as sundews, catch insects with tentacles which spring in a regular pattern from the upper surface of the leaf blades. In fact the tentacles are long glandular hairs. Each gland secretes a large droplet of mucilage, which accounts for the dewy appearance of the leaf. The leaf shines in the sun and this appears to attract insects.

When the insect lands on the leaf, it sticks to the glue exuded by the tentacles and struggles to escape. But by doing so it stimulates the tentacles which bend over the insect's body and cover it with slime,

Venus fly trap
Dionaea muscipula

Pitcher plant
Nepenthes mixta

literally suffocating the prey. Then the tentacles secrete a digestive juice which acts on the soft parts of the insect. When the digestible parts of the prey have been absorbed, the tentacles open again and the insect remains are thrown to the wind. The plant then waits for a new catch.

The dangerous sundew is extremely sensitive to the presence of insects and the reaction of its tentacles is almost immediate and lasts some ten seconds until the insect is totally paralysed.

Darwin, who was particularly interested in these peculiar plants, said that sundews have a particular liking for rump steak, as the smallest piece of it caused a strong reaction in the plant. Even a small piece of meat, or part of an insect's body, or egg white causes the sensitive tentacles to react. Even a minute piece of a human hair, as small as eight ten-thousandths of a gram, placed upon the plant tentacles causes a definite response. The object introduced must contain some proteins—otherwise the plant shows no interest. For instance, it ignores a minute piece of glass, wood or paper.

There are many plants which catch and digest insects using both the leaves and stems for the purpose. One in this group is an Australian native called giant rainbow (*Drosera binata*) because of its large size. Its thread-like narrow leaves and stems are covered in glandular tentacles capable of capturing even large insects. Once the prey is entangled, its flesh is digested by means of a juice secreted by minute glands found on the surface of the plant.

Some insects even help this plant to capture fatter prey. The wingless leaf bug lives in a kind of relationship with the plant, capturing other insects. It feeds itself by extracting nutrients from the bodies of insects captured by the plant but not yet consumed. In other words this tiny bug, which must be immune to the digestive glands of the plant, is permitted to share the prey. As well, this tiny bug attracts other insects and is a kind of live bait. In this peculiar way the plant seems to have a better chance to capture more nutritious prey. The tiny bug itself is not an attractive food for the sundew.

Some insectivorous plants e.g. *Drosophyllum lusitanicum*, have been used in certain areas as a natural flypaper, especially in Portugal. The sticky plants continue to catch insects even when the plants are dead.

Carnivorous Fungi

Not only higher plants but also some fungi are known to consume animals. The first tiny fungi capable of capturing animal prey were discovered in 1888. Such fungi as *Arthobotrys oligospora* are small microscopic creatures, which have minute loops like lassos with which they catch small live nematodes. They then send out special branches known as haustoria which digest and absorb the animal flesh.

In some fungi the trapping loops are composed of three cells which exude a strong adhesive fluid when attacking and capturing prey.

Insectivorous fungi usually live in dung and soil humus.

Giant rainbow
Drosera binata

16.
Other Plant Curiosities

Milk Tree

Venezuela is the home of the interesting tree, *Brosimum galactodendron*, which can be milked like a cow, hence its popular name, the cow tree. The trunk of the tree contains a milky latex, which flows out in large quantities when a notch is cut in its bark. This unusual use of a plant surprised the first explorers. As Humboldt, the German naturalist, said in 1799 when he admired this unique tree:

> Its branches appear dead; but when the trunk is pierced there flows from it a sweet and nourishing milk. It is at the rising of the sun that this vegetable fountain is most abundant. The negroes and natives are seen hastening from all quarters, furnished with large bowls to receive the milk which grows yellow and thickens at its surface. Some empty their bowls under the tree itself, others carry the juice to their children.

Although the taste of the tree milk is not as good as that from a cow as it has a slightly astringent aftertaste, it is still regarded as a delicious drink in many countries.

This useful tree is also planted in other regions of the world. For example, it is a popular tree in India and Sri Lanka. Edwin Menninger, an American naturalist and popular writer, is right in calling it 'the snack bar of the forest'.

There are other trees too which exude a milky sap that can be used as a milk substitute. They include the trees belonging to the genus *Couma*, native to northern South America. When injured they exude enough sap to be used as a milk, hence a popular name for the trees, the cow trees. As this milk has a pleasant and sweetish taste, it is much used by the natives. This 'milk' has even been employed for the production of chewing gum where it serves as a substitute for chicle. These trees are beautiful when in bloom. The most attractive among them is *Couma utilis*, which bears most attractive clusters of pink flowers. Some naturalists regard this plant as the most beautiful tree in the world.

Petrol Plant

Among the many members of the spurge family there is a peculiar plant, *Euphorbia tirucalli*, known as milk-hedge, because of the milky sap it exudes after injury. It often grows as large as a tree and has a very unusual appearance; its branches are leafless and as thin as a pencil, and because

Petrol Plant
Euphorbia tirucalli

of the lack of leaves this succulent plant is often called naked lady. It grows very fast and is commonly cultivated in tropical regions as a boundary for paddy fields, especially in Sri Lanka.

The copious white sap is dangerous to the eyes and causes temporary blindness which may last for days. The plant is often grown in botanic gardens as a curiosity because of its unique pencil-like branches, hence another name being pencil bush.

Petrol plant, formerly regarded as almost useless, has now attracted the attention of scientists. It has been discovered that its dangerous sap or milky juice contains large amounts of hydrocarbons which may be changed into a petrol-like product. This would be a really extraordinary use of a living plant. That our future cars may run on plant material is really an exciting idea, which might be regarded as a fantasy, but it has been calculated that from the plants grown on one hectare, up to 125 barrels of pure petrol can be obtained. We still have to wait for further research results, but certainly the naked lady now deserves more respect.

Fertility Doll

There is a palm (*Hyphaene coriacea*) in East Africa which bears shiny brown fruits about 5 cm long. The fruits are hard and oval shaped which suits the purpose of members of the Turkana tribe in Kenya who make them into dolls. The fruit becomes the head of the doll, to which a goat skin apron is attached. They are made only by mothers who have daughters. The doll is an important gift to a young girl as it is believed to be a talisman bringing good luck and is of special value to a girl who is mature and looking for a husband. The doll her mother gives her has a clean apron and the girl decorates it herself with beads, often given to her by her boyfriend.

The doll must then be given a name, which is usually the name of a best friend. A possible candidate for marriage is chosen, and the young couple refer to the doll as their son. During the dancing ceremonies in the village, when the girl calls her doll's name, it is a signal to her boyfriend and an indirect request for him to approach her and ask for a dance.

The magic doll is always kept around the girl's neck or on her shoulders when outdoors. During the rest of the day and at night the doll is hung on a wall in the sleeping area of the hut.

In the Ashanti region in Ghana, so-called fertility dolls are very popular. These dolls are carved from the wood of the akuaba tree (*Picralima nitida*). They are flat figures resembling a human body, the head of which is large and the rest of the body small. The shape of the figure leaves no doubt which is the figure of a boy. Such dolls are kept under the woman's dress, often hanging from her neck.

An expectant mother wears the appropriate figure, depending upon whether she wants her next child to be a boy or a girl. It is a common belief that the fertility doll has the miraculous power to ensure that a child of the desired sex is born.

A Drink for Men Only

The small tree (*Ilex vomitoria*) is highly esteemed by the American Indians. An extract of the leaves is used as a ceremonial drink by various tribes, especially in a purifying rite before hunting. To prepare the drink, the Indians boil the dried leaves with water for several hours so that a thick, black extract is obtained, usually called black drink. It is regarded in some regions as a liquor for only the strongest men and only the bravest warriors were allowed to drink it.

Some Indian tribes use black drink during important tribal events, especially during harvest festivals. The drink seems to be ideal for purification purposes, since in large doses it causes immediate vomiting, which could be just what is required.

An Indian tribe, the Cultachiches, inhabiting the west bank of the Mississippi River had a peculiar custom of forbidding women this men-only drink. An early Spanish explorer wrote in 1564: 'If by chance the boiling leaves should be uncovered, and a woman should come by in the meantime, they would drink none of it but fling it all away. Likewise while it was cooling and being poured out to drink no woman is allowed to move, or they would pour it all out on the ground and spew up any which they might have drunk, while she would be severely beaten.' When a man preparing the black drink called out: 'Who will drink?', the women present became motionless 'and were they sitting or standing, even on tip-toe, or with one leg raised and the other down, they dared not change their position' until the liquor was cooled and ready to drink. The men explained this 'foolish' behaviour by saying that if the woman did not stand still on hearing the call some evil would enter the liquor which they believed would kill them.

White settlers were puzzled by this peculiar custom, but it is said they also wanted to be classed as brave men so they joined the Indians in their drink. Later they started taking black drink in a more diluted form on a regular basis. When used in the form of an infusion, it has a stimulating effect similar to strong tea or coffee.

Plant of Cannibals

Probably the most macabre use of a plant was related to cannibalism. Human flesh-eating by men was once most common in central Africa,

New Guinea and Melanesia, especially in Fiji. The custom has not ceased even now in some remote regions where it is still being practised. In Papua New Guinea in 1961 a young anthropologist, a member of the Rockefeller family, became a prey of cannibals from the Agat tribe. His body has never been found.

Cannibalism used to be common in Fiji, where special wooden forks were used. Using fingers was avoided as it was believed that touching such meat would cause dreadful disease. The main source of food were prisoners of war. One of the inhabitants of a Fiji village said: 'I have eaten human flesh when I was a small boy. I believed it was pig's meat. But later I learned that I was wrong as I noticed that such feasts in which I could participate only took place after the deadly fight. We had special plants in the leaves of which we covered bodies before we placed them in an oven'. It has been discovered that the plant used in this manner was a member of the potato family, *Solanum anthropophagorum*, known as cannibal's tomato, because its red fruits resemble tomatoes. The specific name 'anthropophagorum' was well chosen as in Greek it means 'the eating of men'.

Early missionaries who wanted to show the natives a different way of life and convert them to Christianity, were often victims of cannibals. According to L. de Marden, in 1867, in one of the Fiji islands, a white missionary named Thomas Baker was killed and eaten by cannibals. A somewhat macabre story is associated with this event, which is still remembered in the island. As the cannibals had never seen shoes they tried to cook Mr Baker together with his foot cover. Although they cooked the body for many days to make the 'meat' tender, the 'feet' were still tough. No wonder that there is a saying in Fiji 'Eat the boots of Mr Baker!'

Illustrations

Acknowledgements of Illustrations

The publishers and the authors would like to thank the following for permission to use their photographs.

Huey W. Hachette, Paris p. 133

Inkata Press, Mount Waverley, Victoria pp. 26, 62

Ivanovic Ion, Cairns, Queensland p. 58

Professor H.C.D. de Wit, Agricultural University, Wageningen, The Netherlands pp. 85, 88, 89, 123, 125, 126, 145, 153, 155.

Index

An asterisk indicates an illustration